The Sonneveld House

Contents

5 **Foreword**
Rudy Voogd and Meindert Booij

7 **Introduction**
Kristin Feireiss

10 **A Tailor-Made Suit**
Barbara Laan

34 **The Dijkzigt Villa Park**
Elly Adriaansz

44 **The Sonneveld House
The design history within the oeuvre of Brinkman and
Van der Vlugt and in relation to contemporaries**
Joris Molenaar

66 **The Garden of The Sonneveld House
Part of an unusual ensemble**
Eric Blok and Birgit Lang

73 **The Sonneveld House**
Photography by Jannes Linders

89 Telephones
93 Kitchen curtains
108 Wall clock
109 Dinner service
112 Vases
113 Staircase window
116 Rugs
117 Linoleum
123 Sanitary fittings
126 Toilet requisites
127 Tabouret
Jojanneke Clarijs and Mienke Simon Thomas

128 **The Interior of The Sonneveld House, Then and Now**
Barbara Laan and Sjoerd Wierda

146 **Reconstruction of an Atmospheric Colour Scheme**
Lisette Kappers and Joris Molenaar

152 **A Modern Villa from 1933 in 2001
'As if nothing has happened'**
Willem Jan Paijmans and Joris Molenaar

Foreword

The year 1923 witnessed the establishment of a foundation that aimed 'to promote the spiritual and physical well-being of the people of Rotterdam' – Stichting Bevordering van Volkskracht. Building was already an area on which Volkskracht focused from the start. The Volkskracht board has always been broadly based, representing as many social and cultural sectors as possible in its portfolios. The first member of the board with the building and architecture portfolio was the architect L.C. van der Vlugt.

Over the years Volkskracht has made many contributions to the construction and interior of buildings of socio-cultural importance, as well as funding museums, exhibitions and publications in the field of building and architecture. It has recently subsidised several restoration projects of designs by the Rotterdam firm of architects Brinkman and Van der Vlugt. These are authentic monuments of Rotterdam, such as Feijenoord Stadium and the Van der Leeuw House (the house in the Kralingse Plaslaan that belonged to the visionary member of the Van Nelle firm).

During the construction of the Maas Boulevard, Volkskracht became involved in moving and restoring the inn In den Rustwat, including taking over ownership of these premises to guarantee the continuity of the management of the restored tavern. This led to the Stichting Volkskracht Historische Monumenten in 1984. The aim of this foundation as laid down in the articles of association is to purchase and restore classified monuments. The premises that have been acquired by the foundation in the course of the last few years are rented or made available to users that meet the criteria of the Volkskracht aims.

Rotterdam does not have a reputation as a city with a wealth of historic monuments, but it does have a number of monuments – 'young monuments', as they are sometimes called – from the Dutch Modernist Movement, such as the Van der Leeuw House. During the restoration of the Van der Leeuw House, the idea was raised of restoring it as a museum home and as an example of avant-garde architecture in the 1930s, but the owner of the Van der Leeuw House had other plans.

This was one of the reasons why the foundation wanted to add a young monument to the portfolio.

Among the potential candidates was The Sonneveld House. Sonneveld was one of the directors of Van Nelle. Like Van der Leeuw, he had his house designed by the Brinkman and Van der Vlugt firm of architects.

The Sonneveld House passed into the hands of the Belgian State in the 1950s, when it was used as a residence and for receptions by the consul. The development of modern means of communication made Belgian consular activities in Rotterdam virtually redundant in the 1990s. The real estate could be abandoned. Partly thanks to the diplomatic support of the Rotterdam local authority, the Belgian State turned out to be prepared to transfer The Sonneveld House to Volkskracht. The board of Volkskracht has happy memories of the contacts with Ambassador Willems, who knew the house well, as it was his father who had lived in The Sonneveld House as the first consul general of Belgium.

At the moment when Volkskracht acquired The Sonneveld House, it was unclear how it would be restored and used. The board of Volkskracht had the expertise required for a professional restoration, but it was necessary to cooperate with a partner in the running of the museum home. When Volkskracht started to look for partners who might be able to play a role in the future plans and management of the premises, the response of the Netherlands Architecture Institute was extremely enthusiastic. This neighbouring institute proved to be an excellent partner.

The management of the project of restoring The Sonneveld House was assumed within the Stichting Volkskracht Historische Monumenten by Joop van der Leeuw and Hans Boot. They cooperated intensively with Mariet Willinge and Barbara Laan from the Netherlands Architecture Institute. Wim Crouwel unselfishly brought his knowledge and experience to many discussions. Information sometimes came from an unexpected quarter too, such as from Leonard Kooij, the grandson of the first occupants. Joris Molenaar from Molenaar & Van Winden architecten performed the extremely multi-faceted role of architect. The construction and restoration work was in the hands of the subcontractor Schakel & Schrale bv.

The enthusiasm and dedication of these and many others have made an enormous success of The Sonneveld House, as this splendid book shows. We are very grateful to them for their efforts, and are convinced that many will come to share our gratitude over the years.

Rudy Voogd
Chairman of Stichting Bevordering van Volkskracht

Meindert Booij
Chairman of Stichting Volkskracht Historische Monumenten

5

L.C. van der Vlugt,
The Sonneveld House
(12 Jongkindstraat), 1932-1933

Introduction

It is not for nothing that the architecture of Brinkman and Van der Vlugt is included in major surveys of twentieth-century architectural history. The impressive factory premises for the Van Nelle firm with its characteristic silhouette, its mushroom columns and its glass curtain walls, is world famous. When the famous French architect Le Corbusier visited the Netherlands in January 1932 to give a series of lectures, he was met by the man who had commissioned the building, Kees van der Leeuw, and 'his architect', Leen van der Vlugt. Le Corbusier called the factory 'the most beautiful spectacle of the modern era' and 'a delightful proof of the life that is coming, of the beautiful, unconditional purity'.

Van der Vlugt designed The Sonneveld House for one of the directors of the Van Nelle factory. It is on the list of Dutch Historic Monuments and its present owner, the Stichting Volkskracht Historische Monumenten, has put its management in the hands of the Netherlands Architecture Institute. This generous Rotterdam foundation has made it possible to fully restore the interior design, furniture and fittings of the house and to make it suitable for museum and educational activities. Visitors to the museum can be professionally guided around the house using the audiotour and be introduced to the value of the building and its interior. An impressive video presentation emphasises the importance of Van der Vlugt's architecture and demonstrates how the restoration of the premises and interior has been carried out.

The Netherlands Architecture Institute wants to present The Sonneveld House to the public as a museum home on a scale of 1:1. The aim is to introduce visitors to this building as an example of a functionalist home. The whole house has been furnished as it was on the date of completion in 1933. The decision to reconstruct this *Gesamtkunstwerk* was taken by the restoration commission under its inspiring chair, Wim Crouwel. This commission consists of representatives of Volkskracht, the Collection Department of the Netherlands Architecture Institute, and Molenaar & Van Winden architecten. I am grateful to the members of the commission for their dedication to achieving our common goal and to making a success of it. The Sonneveld House is an important acquisition for the museum world not least because it contains many of the original pieces of steel tubular furniture and lamps. They are on loan from the Sonneveld family through the Foundation for the Preservation of the Interior of The Sonneveld House. We are also grateful for the loans and donations by private collectors and by large and small Dutch museums and institutions.

This richly illustrated publication on The Sonneveld House will provide the museum visitor with a thorough insight into the design of the house and the urban planning situation in which it arose. There is ample coverage of the client and his family and of modern life around 1930. Various aspects of the process of restoration of the building and interior are dealt with in a number of contributions. There is also discussion of aspects of the interior decoration and the works of (applied) art on display there. The book as a whole is an ode to a very special architecture.

Kristin Feireiss
Director Netherlands Architecture Institute

South and East elevation, 1933

Sitting area in Mr Sonneveld's study
with the living room and
Mrs Sonneveld's desk in the
background, 1933

A Tailor-Made Suit

Barbara Laan

A remarkable enterprise

The house of the Sonneveld family in the Jongkind-straat in Rotterdam has become one of the icons of the Nieuwe Bouwen and Nieuwe Wonen movements.[1] It is a model of a modern home which has become normal nowadays, but which was progressive in 1933 from the angle of both domestic comfort and design. The decision to want to live in this house with its vast rooms, advanced domestic technology and refined details does not seem so strange today. However, it became clear in the course of the inquiry, especially during the many discussions with people who knew the Sonneveld family well, that it was by no means so natural to want to live in a 'modern' home in the early 1930s. On the contrary, many viewed it as a 'remarkable enterprise'.[2] Modernist architecture was not the obvious choice for a prime-location middle-class residence that it was for hospitals, factories and working-class housing. And the members of the family were viewed with astonishment because

they left almost all of their belongings behind in the old house. The decision to live in a modern home called for an attitude orientated towards the future, a modern way of life. The question that particularly intrigued me was what led the Sonnevelds to take such an important decision and with it to undergo a fundamental change in terms of taste and life-style.

Domestic taste is not only an aesthetic statement; it is also an expression of social identity, and for many people of personal identity as well. Domestic taste is therefore connected, irrespective of the type of home and interior that you want, with decisions about the city, the neighbourhood and the street where you want to live, and in the last resort with the domestic articles with which you surround yourself too.

The Sonnevelds opted for a good neighbourhood in Rotterdam, not for Wassenaar or another high-class district. They opted for a new building instead of an old one, and instead of a brick house with a gable roof they chose a modern 'white villa' and an interior to match. That interior consisted of upholstery, furniture, lamps, a wireless set with speakers, a gramophone,

1   The use of the term Nieuwe Wonen for functionalist homes in a Modernist style was introduced in the publication: T. Eliëns (ed.), *Het Nieuwe Wonen in Nederland 1924-1936*, Rotterdam 1990, 9.

2   Interview with Mrs M.H.F. (Beb) Witteveen-Jansen, a friend of the youngest daughter Gé from a lower class at school, on 7 December 1999.

Mrs Sonneveld and Mr Sonneveld
in the garden, with the Westersingel
houses in the background, ca. 1933

Engagement photograph of
Mr and Mrs Sonneveld, 1910

Puck and Gé in the garden of the
house on the Heemraadssingel, 1926

Interior of the house on the
Heemraadssingel: the maid Martha
brings a letter from Mr Sonneveld,
who is on a business trip, 1925

fixed electric clocks, a telephone with internal and external lines, office articles, (glass) tableware and vases.[3] The splendid Steinway grand piano was new when it was purchased.[4] The only articles that we know or may suppose to have been brought from the old house were books, clothes and a few small personal belongings, as well as works of art. The latter included the beautiful sculpture of a seated lion, designed by the sculptor John Rädecker,[5] and a number of maritime and river scenes by painters like Willem Bastiaan Tholen. These works of art were incorporated in the interior with specially designed frames for the paintings and a black rectangular socle for the sculpture.[6]

I gradually became convinced that the Sonnevelds' decision was an unusual one for the average middle-class family in the early 1930s, but a logical one in their particular case. The new attitude implicit in the modern architecture and interior proved to correspond closely to the personalities of the couple – at least, to the picture that emerged from interviews, photographs and biographical documents.[7] Before opting for Nieuwe Bouwen, the family will have become gradually accustomed to functionalist architecture with its literally cold materials like steel and its openness and emptiness, because such an affinity is a precondition of being able to make the transition to modern design.

Dreams of the future of new citizens of Rotterdam

Every Tuesday evening the entire family gathered around a table cluttered with floor plans in the old house on the Heemraadssingel, the eldest daughter Puck recalled.[8] Her face, like those of her father Bertus, her mother Gesine, and her sister Gé,[9] was probably illuminated by the dining room lamp that can be seen hanging above the centre of the table in a film fragment from 1925,[10] next to the bell-rope. The architect Leen van der Vlugt was a regular visitor to The Sonneveld Household between 1929 and 1933 to explain and discuss his plans for the new home in the Jongkind-straat.

The house on the Heemraadssingel – a beautiful wide canal flanked by trees in front of resplendent mansions,[11] had a front and a back room separated by partition doors. The use of the front room as a sitting room or salon and the back room as a dining room was traditional. The terraced houses on the Heemraads-singel were built of brick. Number 158, where the Sonneveld family lived, and the immediate neighbours had a stepped gable. They were to move from a dark house with its impractical arrangement and old-fashioned interior to a spacious, light and empty one, fitted with every modern convenience and surrounded by marvellous products of the industry of the day.

The wide green strip on the
Heemraadssingel, ca. 1928

The house on the Heemraadssingel,
ca. 1928

Puck in front of the entrance to
the house on the Heemraadssingel,
1925

3 Some of the glass must have been purchased when they moved or slightly before then in view of the design dates of around 1930. With thanks to Marcel Brouwer of Christies for his help in identifying the designs.

4 The eldest daughter, Puck, played modern music as well as Chopin. She was very musical. As a secondary school pupil she was advised by the music school to go on to the conservatory. The Music Schools Association for Music, Rotterdam and District Branch, wrote this in 1929, according to L. Kooij, *De bewoners van huis Sonneveld*, Hellendoorn/Rotterdam 1999, 4.

5 The sculpture by John Rädecker is of a seated lion. It is executed in diabase, a black mineral with green veins that is difficult to work because it is so hard. Mrs Sonneveld visited the sculptor's workshop in 1925. It was the 25th anniversary of her husband's service with Van Nelle. He was offered a grand party in the modern Pschorr dance hall on the Coolsingel. It is not known whether he was presented with the sculpture on that occasion. Mrs Sonneveld described her visit on 5 November 1925 on a postcard. Preservation of the Interior of Sonneveld House Collection.

6 A drawing of the socle was kept, and the delivery of frames for paintings is also known from the archival documents. The sculpture itself remained in the family, so that a cast could be made for the museum. The Preservation of the Interior of Sonneveld House Collection also kept a painting frame.

7 Some of the sources belong to the Preservation of the Interior of Sonneveld House Collection; others are the property of the grandson Leonard Kooij.

8 This interview was conducted by Joris Molenaar on 20 December 1995.

9 Albertus Hendrikus Sonneveld, nicknamed Bertus, was born in Vlaardingen on 6 February 1885. Gesine Grietje Bos was born in Tubbergen (Twente) on 3 August 1886. Their eldest daughter, Magdalena (Magda for short, nicknamed Puck), was born in the Burgemeester Meineszlaan 106a in Rotterdam on 5 July 1913. Most people called the youngest daughter Gé, from Gesine. She was born at the same address on 16 December 1920.

10 The film was made on the occasion of the 25th anniversary of Mr Sonneveld's employment with the Van Nelle company. It shows the family life of his wife, two daughters and resident servant at a time when he was himself in the United States on a business trip.

11 G. Peet, *Burgermansgepruts. 100 jaar Heemraadssingel, 1900-2000*, Rotterdam 2000.

Gé with the dog Teddy in
Mr Sonneveld's Plymouth de luxe,
1930s

Mrs Sonneveld, Puck and Gesine on
the beach at Scheveningen, 1925

Mr Sonneveld (l) inspecting tobacco
leaves in America, 1924

In 1906, when Bertus Sonneveld had just served six years in the employ of the Van Nelle company, he sketched a pipe dream – on the occasion of the firm's jubilee – in which the city of Rotterdam figures in the year 2006. Rotterdam and its port would grow to become the 'largest trading post in Western Europe', he wrote in the anniversary newspaper.[12] This contribution was to prove characteristic of the personality of Mr Sonneveld, his confidence in the future of Rotterdam, and his unshakable belief in commerce and its role in the growth of the world economy. The company of 'The Heirs of Widow J. van Nelle' where Sonneveld began as a young assistant in 1900 gave him the opportunity to rise to the rank of deputy general manager by 1919. When the firm became a limited company in 1935, he was appointed business director of the tobacco division, a position he was to occupy until his retirement in 1950. Thanks to the favourable bonus system for directors, in spite of the world economic crisis of 1929 he was wealthy enough to be able to afford a new detached house with furniture and fittings.[13]

The young Bertus Sonneveld's vision of the future – he was in his early twenties in 1906 – also illustrates his propensity for grand gestures. It is therefore hardly surprising that 'the land of unlimited possibilities', the United States, was his great model. After travelling to the United States for the first time in 1909 at the age

of twenty-four, he registered upon his return as a resident of Rotterdam.[14] 'Travelling salesman' was the description of his profession that he gave to the clerk of the register, and with boundless enthusiasm he gave as his place of departure 'New York'. Sonneveld's language betrayed his regular visits abroad: he regularly used Anglicisms, at least in his correspondence. For instance, he referred to the tobacco crop by its English term. He spent many months a year travelling in the West and South of the United States to sample, purchase and arrange the shipping of tobacco for the Van Nelle company. Not only his use of language, but also his taste for conveniences was also clearly influenced by North America. As a result of his many journeys he had become extremely attached to such 'American comfort'. He sailed on the ocean liners of the White Star Line and the Cunard Line, and regularly slept in luxurious American hotels, such as the Hotel Pennsylvania in New York, which with 2,200 rooms was the largest of its kind at the time (1924). His American taste was apparent not only in tobacco and music but also in cars. In the 1930s he drove a Plymouth de luxe, and later a Chevrolet. He wanted room for two cars in the garage of his new house: one for his own car, and one for his wife Gesine's two-seater Packard convertible. Yet in spite of the wealth acquired through his own efforts and his urge to show it off, he was above

The Sonneveld House under
construction, summer 1932

Mr Sonneveld in the garden,
ca. 1933

all known as a modest and cultured man with a genuine interest in the ups and downs of his fellow human beings. He commanded respect as a self-made businessman with Van Nelle, but he was not authoritarian. Thanks to his simple background and the fact that he was himself responsible for his general development, he moved easily among people from all walks of life: the factory workers, the Van Nelle partners, and the US tobacco planters. The common ground that someone like Van der Vlugt probably shared with Sonneveld was an exceptional interest in everything connected with technology. While Van der Vlugt was sketching the design for the new Van Nelle factory in Overschie, Sonneveld was visiting factories in Germany.[15]

Although it is not known exactly what he saw there, he was evidently interested in the tools and machinery for the production of tobacco: benches for cutting tobacco leaves, transport belts to carry it to other parts of the factory, and fully automatic cigarette machines for the production of cigarettes from picking up and cutting the paper to size to the packaging of the rolled and sealed cigarette.

Technology was one of his preoccupations in his private life as well. He started photography in 1920, and bought his first film camera in 1926, but his interests extended beyond film and photography to communication technology. In his bookcase 'Introduction to art history' rubbed shoulders with books on radio-

12   'It is the year 2006. It is a fine day in May, and a huge crowd of people are passing through the streets of Maasstad, the name given to Rotterdam after its extension to the North Sea. Foreigners from every corner of the world come here to trade the different products of their lands in the largest trading post in Western Europe, which is what Maasstad has gradually become.' In a later passage he describes what the buildings in the city look like: 'mainly 15-storey blocks of houses on both sides of the street'. Rotterdam Municipal Archive, Archives of the heirs of Widow J. Van Nelle, inv. no. 3144: A.H.S. 'Fantastische Toekomstdroomen', *De Rijzende Hoop* (centenary magazine), 21 April 1906, 3.

13   J. Molenaar, 'Huis sonneveld. Bron van atmosferische nieuwzakelijke interieurkunst', *Jaarboek Cuypersgenootschap 2000. Achter gesloten deuren. Bronnen voor interieurhistorisch onderzoek*, 16 (2001), 70-83.

14   Marinus Wisse Sonneveld and Magdalena Cornelia Klein, Bertus's parents, lived in Vlaardingen when he was born. Bertus grew up in Willemstad with a childless uncle and aunt because the family (with a total of four sons) could not pay for him to attend primary school. He moved to Rotterdam in 1899, and was taken on by Van Nelle as the youngest assistant in 1900. At first he lived at 12a Gerrit Jan Mulderstraat.

Puck on the terrace, behind the house,
1933

Gé on the terrace of the outdoor room,
1933

telegraphy. Perhaps it was his meticulous nature that paved the way for his predilection for technology – although precision was a characteristic of the entire family. 'There was a cult of tidiness in The Sonneveld House', according to Liesbeth Quartero, who often visited the family in her childhood.[16] Mrs Sonneveld was also very precision-minded. This could be seen not only from the tidy impression that the house in the Jongkindstraat always made, but also from the spick and span state of the house on the Heemraadssingel. Though the interior was fairly cluttered, there was never a crumpled or untidy piece of fabric or magazine. Everything was tidied up and put away immediately after use. Even the daughters shared this apparently innate love of tidiness. Or was it the result of the firm hand with which Mrs Sonneveld not only ran her household but also managed her family?

The transition to Nieuwe Wonen was probably a question of comfort for Mr Sonneveld. He was interested in American things, in economy, efficiency and technology. He liked clever inventions and practical refinements. He really *loved* gadgets, especially the ones which made life easier, such as lifts, telephones, cigarette lighters, ocean liners and zeppelins. Mrs Sonneveld shared his great affinity with the utility of objects. But she was first and foremost a practical woman who did not like wasting time, and above all

money. She wanted the cooking in her household to be done with gas, and not with the allegedly cleaner electricity which was recommended for that reason in many Neue Sachlichkeit publications. Cooking by gas was cheaper and faster! Mrs Sonneveld was a resolute, independent woman who was used to coping on her own when her husband was away for months at a time. She probably did not know the theory of the famous US engineer F.W. Taylor, unless it was from the local newspaper in which the house of Van der Leeuw was discussed in detail. It described the technical refinements, the practical use of a sliding partition, and the 'Taylor system'.[17] Taylor had devised a system to increase labour productivity around the turn of the century. He used time and motion studies to analyse the process of production in factories in order to step up efficiency. His system of rationalisation was later applied to housekeeping around 1915 by an engineer's wife, Christine Fredericks.[18] The idea of saving time will have appealed to Mrs Sonneveld.

The choice of Nieuwe Wonen must have appealed to her in another way too. Mrs Sonneveld had a taste for luxury and opulence, which was displayed in the way she dressed. When she went out she regularly wore a hat with a hat-pin. She never went out without an elegant cloak, often ankle-length and sometimes with a fur collar, even if she was only on her way to feed the

Graf Zeppelin airship lands in
Rotterdam, 18 June 1932

Mrs Sonneveld in the Grindelwald
with Puck and Gé, ca. 1928

swans in the lake near Museum Boijmans.[19] She always wore jewellery. Mr Sonneveld's clothes were generally elegant too, even a little frivolous. He might go to the coast wearing a suit with a high collar, waistcoat and a handkerchief in his breast-pocket, but the floppy brim of his hat betrayed a certain flamboyance.

Mrs Sonneveld was clearly attached to status symbols. As a resident on the Heemraadssingel, she must have been well aware of how far she had climbed up the social ladder. That rise can be seen from the succession of streets in which she had lived in Rotterdam. Her first home was in the Bellevoystraat, one of the many streets running from north to south just west of the triangle in the old part of Rotterdam. They had been

rapidly constructed by property developers for a mass of new Rotterdammers at the end of the nineteenth century. It was not a working-class district, but an unpretentious one where the lower ranks of the civil service lived, for example. The top floor was small, and the houses in this street were poorly constructed.[20] Besides, it was a bare street with small workshops and businesses. The house in the Burgemeester Meineszlaan, where she moved after marrying Bertus in 1912, was already more stylish. The street was wider, consisting mainly of homes, and there was some greenery. But the Heemraadssingel was the real thing. This street, with its canal flanked by trees, its paths and small parks, was so wide that you could not see into the

15 Sonneveld went on a business trip in Germany in 1927, visiting Berlin and other cities.
16 Interview with Liesbeth Telders-Quartero on 11 August 1999.

17 Anonymous, 'Excursie naar het modernste huis van Rotterdam', Rotterdam Municipal Archive, Van Vollenhoven 23 October to 9 November 1929, Rotterdam 211, 39-40.

18 On the Taylor system and housekeeping books see: M. Wilke, 'Kennis en kunde' in: R. Oldenziel and C. Bouw (eds), *Schoon genoeg. Huisvrouwen en huishoudtechnologie in Nederland 1898-1998*, [Amsterdam 1998], 59-90.

19 The present site of the field of shells and

the asphalt square of the Museumpark by the OMA firm of architects and landscape architect Yves Brunier, who worked with OMA at the time.

20 Gesine Sonneveld, née Bos, lived at 67b Bellevoystraat and taught handicraft. Her father was apparently able to pay for an education for his daughter. Her parents, Aldert Harms Bos and Rinske Geerts Prangsma, came from Friesland. Aldert Bos was in the police force and was stationed in Overijssel. Gesine was born in Tubbergen, but grew up in Vroomshoop. In 1898 the family registered at the Rotterdam Local Authority as being from Deventer.

Gé on the sofa in the living room,
1930s

homes of the neighbours on the other side. This was where well-to-do Rotterdammers lived, most of whom belonged to the old upper crust. There were doctors, businessmen and directors of dockside companies, such as Mr Vinke, the director of the Vroom & Dreesmann department store chain, Mr Henkes, who owned a distillery, and the director of the famous glass and porcelain shop Jungerhans. Kees van der Leeuw, one of the partners in Van Nelle, had also lived there for a short spell.

Her next move was to the fringe of the Land van Hoboken, a name that everyone in Rotterdam knew and loved for the romantic greenery surrounding the old classicistic house of the rich harbour industrialist.[21] It was a beautiful spot with a view of the park and a hint of the water of the Maas behind the Westzeedijk. Mrs Sonneveld seemed to have a sixth sense for the far-ranging consequences of opting for modern design. She realised the attractiveness of a modern set of glasses in the dining room showcase. Leerdam glass was a common name among culturally interested circles. Mrs Sonneveld ordered a set, including cham-

pagne glasses, Annagrün glasses for Rhine wine, and glasses for red wine, (the 'Servies B (smooth)' from 1917) from the architect K.P.C. de Bazel. The set for water, designed by Cornelis de Lorm, also came from the Leerdam glass factory. She also had a set of globular vases and the square vase, and probably an enormous unicum vase with *tincraquelé* rings by Andries Copier. The new house must have offered Mrs Sonneveld an opportunity to make the acquaintance of a cultural élite before whom she could parade her social identity as a director's wife. And the consistency in the complete interior design imposed by Nieuwe Bouwen also fitted her rigid personality to a tee.

See and be seen
The floor plan of The Sonneveld House was an open one. This means that the shape of the rooms and their position with regard to one another were not in principle tied to a conventional pattern as they had been on the Heemraadssingel. That house had two bays behind the front wall, a narrow one for the hall and

Puck and Gé on the sofa in the living room, 1930s

movement through the house, and a wide one for the front and back rooms. All the same, many familiar elements were introduced into the Sonneveld family's new house as well. This is logical, since the floor plan and the spatial composition reflect the Sonneveld family's domestic requirements. Books with photographs and floor plans of middle-class homes from the first decades of the twentieth century and books of advice on how to arrange a home provide countless examples of the conventions of the time.

A striking feature of the new house is the situation of the living room on the first floor. This raises the family above its surroundings and offers it a splendid view of the surroundings. To live upstairs was modern, and yet not modern. Many functionally designed houses have the living room on the first floor. This is the case in Le Corbusier's villas as a result of the pilotis (the series of columns used to raise the building above ground level), as well as in the house that Van der Vlugt designed for Van der Leeuw. Living upstairs has long-standing roots in the Netherlands, where the damp ground made it wise to live at any rate above

the basement level. The basement was good enough for the kitchen and the other utility rooms, and was partly underground. Living on the first floor was not unprecedented in Rotterdam; a number of houses were built from 1900 on in which this was the case, as various floor plans by the Rotterdam architect Verheul show.[22]

When it comes to making one's entrance, The Sonneveld House is modern in appearance, although modelled around the conventional ingredients. The route that residents and visitors have to follow is unexpected, with all kinds of bends and turnings, and it is monumental in a modern way. It starts modestly with a garden path and a small, enclosed front terrace at the left-hand corner of the house. The storm porch and the entrance hall are dark because the black marble wall absorbs the little light that enters through

21   This Villa Dijkzigt was built in 1856 by J.F. Metzelaar. It is the present-day premises of the Natuurmuseum.

22   J.H.W. Leliman, *Het stadswoonhuis in Nederland*, The Hague 1920; J.G. Wattjes, *Moderne Nederlandsche villa's en landhuizen*, Amsterdam 1931.

The library and beside the fireplace the
wood lift, 1933

the small windows. This area is somewhat oppressive
through its elongated shape and the wall overhang, but
it also has something intimate, mainly thanks to the
warm, yellow light from the modern Philinea lamps on
the ceiling.

Those privileged enough to ascend the wide spiral
staircase immediately feel that they are important
guests. In a word, the staircase is enchanting. The cylin-
drical walls are a creamy white. The light falls through
the etched glass of the staircase windows. The optimal
experience of the spatial effect is at the top of the staircase, where the stairs lead the way around a partly
imaginary axis and with an elegant curve. And then
there are the handrails: they wind their way up like
shiny chrome streamers. This forms a major contrast
to the dark, long and narrow corridor with many doors
into which the staircase leads, affording a moment to

recover – but a brief one, because when you enter
the living area the duskiness of this corridor gives
way to a flood of light and space, like going onto the
topmost deck of an ocean liner. The living area was
completely bathed in sunlight: the apotheosis of the
route.

The succession of rooms and zones is in line with
a practice which was considered appropriate for the
life-style of a rich élite and which was also recommended for bourgeois homes of a lower status. Home
guidance manuals from the beginning of the twentieth
century contain mainly practical advice, such as the
use of a storm porch for protection from rain and wind,
or the need for a wardrobe to store outdoor clothes,
preferably with a mirror, because 'for the visitors, and
especially for the ladies, it is agreeable to be able to
add the finishing touch to their hair or dress before

Living room with view through to
dining room, 1933

greeting the hostess'.[23] Even in the late thirties, a few of them were still recommending the use of a waiting room where surprise guests could wait if they had asked for an appointment. This was particularly common in the case of visits 'to make acquaintance', like those of both sets of parents of an engaged couple, according to the manuals of etiquette.[24]

The entrance hall of The Sonneveld House contained a two-seater bench, which should probably be seen as

a relic of this traditional custom of being able to offer visitors a place to sit down. There was also a mirror with a shelf for the clothes brush and handbag.

These recommendations on waiting rooms and asking for an appointment, on rituals of arrival and touching up one's appearance, assume that the household in question kept one or more servants. It was very common to have a servant in the 1920s and 1930s.[25]

23   J. Wils, *Het woonhuis, Vol. II Indeeling en inrichting*, Amsterdam 1923, 29.

24   A. Groskamp-ten Have, *Hoe hoort het eigenlijk?*, Amsterdam 1939, 41. On home manuals and instructions for interiors contained in them see: F. van Burkom and K. Gaillard, 'Droom en daad in de woninginrichting. Een gesprek over de waarde van woonadviesboeken als historische bron', *Jaarboek Cuypersgenootschap 2000. Achter gesloten deuren. Bronnen voor interieur-historisch onderzoek*, 16 (2001), 102-120. Many of

Mrs Sonneveld's habits and views that are known from interviews are perfectly in tune with the prescriptions in etiquette manuals such as that by A. Groskamp-ten Have. On the tradition of these manuals see: B.P.M. Dongelmans, 'Comme il faut. Etiquetteboeken in de negentiende eeuw', *De Negentiende Eeuw*, 23 (1999) 2, 89-123.

25   B. Henkes and H. Oosterhof, *Kaatje ben je boven? Leven en werken van Nederlandse dienstbodes 1900-1940*, Nijmegen 1985, 14-21.

Replica of a sculpture made by
John Rädecker in 1925

Many Dutch households had at least one.[26] Two servants were permanently employed in the Jongkindstraat, and they lived in. They each had a room of their own to which they could retire after evening tea, and they shared a bathroom with a bath. The Rotterdammers talked a lot about this luxurious facility at the time, but an interview with one of the servants revealed that what made the most impression was the speaker in corporated in the built-in radio.[27] Entirely in accordance with the convention in large households of the day, the servants' quarters were strictly separated from the living quarters.[28] This was generally considered to be the ideal situation because it afforded the occupants the most privacy. The separation between servants and occupants went so far that there was a separate servants' staircase, a luxury which by no means every rich family with a new home could afford. This staircase connected the servants' and tradesmen's entrance with the servants' areas such as the garage, where the chauffeur started Mr Sonneveld's car in the morning to warm it up, the servants' corridor where the laundry troughs stood and into which the copper ran, and the servants' rooms.[29] The servants' staircase also provided access to the pantry and stores in the cellar and the kitchen and serving room on the first floor.

There was a sign on the outside wall saying: 'deliveries here' with the times at which deliveries could not be made during lunch and the evening meal. After someone rang, the servant upstairs in the kitchen picked up the telephone to see who it was. She then pressed a button to open the door and to put out the light that showed her at which door the bell had been rung.[30] When she had taken in the delivery, it could be transported by means of the electric lift, which

Living room with a sculpture by
John Rädecker and a painting by
Willem Bastiaan Tholen, 1933

26 Many of them came from Germany, like
the dedicated Martha, the loyal servant of the
Sonneveld family. She also lived in with the family
on the Heemraadssingel. She was only free in
the evenings. German servants were very popular
in the relatively rich Netherlands (which had not
been impoverished by the First World War)
because they had a reputation for being thorough,
hard-working and well brought up girls. Martha
Karl came from Varel near Oldenburg in Nieder-
sachsen, just across the border near Groningen.
Many German servants came from there in the
1920s. See: B. Henkes, *Heimat in Holland: Duitse
dienstmeisjes 1920-1950* (Ph.D. thesis 1995).

27 According to Mrs Den Engelsen-Schreuder
on 19 March 1999. Adriana den Engelsen-
Schreuder worked for the Sonneveld family from
1934 to 1936. The interview with her yielded a
wealth of information about how Mrs Sonneveld's
household functioned. The servants were allowed

to take turns to go home for the weekend once a
fortnight. Shortly before or soon after the move
to the new house in May or June 1933, a second
German servant, Josephine Müller (known as Fini)
was taken on besides Martha. Jeanne Schreuder
was taken on when Martha returned to Germany in
that year to take care of a sick parent.

28 J.H.W. Leliman, *Het stadswoonhuis in
Nederland*, The Hague 1920; J.G. Wattjes,
Moderne Nederlandsche villa's en landhuizen,
Amsterdam 1931.

29 The Sonneveld family's laundry was done
by the C.D. Borgh laundry service, Bellevoystraat
69-75. Interview with Mrs Adriana den Engelsen-
Schreuder on 19 March 1999.

30 The research on the functioning of the
domestic appliances was carried out by Molenaar
& Van Winden architecten in collaboration with
Sjoerd Wierda.

Entrance hall with mirror, hatrack
and bench, 1933

The kitchen with the table where
the servants had their meals, 1933

went to the kitchen (upstairs) and the cellar. Food that could be kept for some time was stored in the pantry; wine was kept in the wine cellar. The servants were responsible for keeping the house clean – a considerable task in view of the many reflecting surfaces and the large amount of daylight and artificial light in the house. There was a lot of cleaning to do, apart from the regular polishing of the 144-piece silver cutlery, a job that occupied two servants for a whole day. Everything had to shine, every item of chrome furniture and every knob on every cupboard and door, window latches, handrails and everything else that was in high-gloss chrome.

Besides keeping the house clean, the servants provided the meals in The Sonneveld House, except for the meat, which was roasted by Mrs Sonneveld herself. Then one of them served at table in a spotless white

apron. When Mrs Sonneveld wanted something she rang by pressing a button in the dining table and not, as was common, by means of a cord hanging above the table. This button activated a buzzer in the kitchen, where the servants ate at their own small table. This table in particularly was appreciated because it afforded such a lovely view.[31]

The Sonneveld House is conceived in a grandiose way when it comes to receiving guests. This is quite in keeping with the allure that the couple evidently wanted. Once a visitor had reached the opening of the living room on the first floor, he found himself surrounded on

31 The small table and chairs were also viewed in a positive light in the contemporary literature. See: K. Limperg, G.J. Meyers and R. Lotgering-Hillebrand, *Keukens*, Rotterdam 1935, 39.

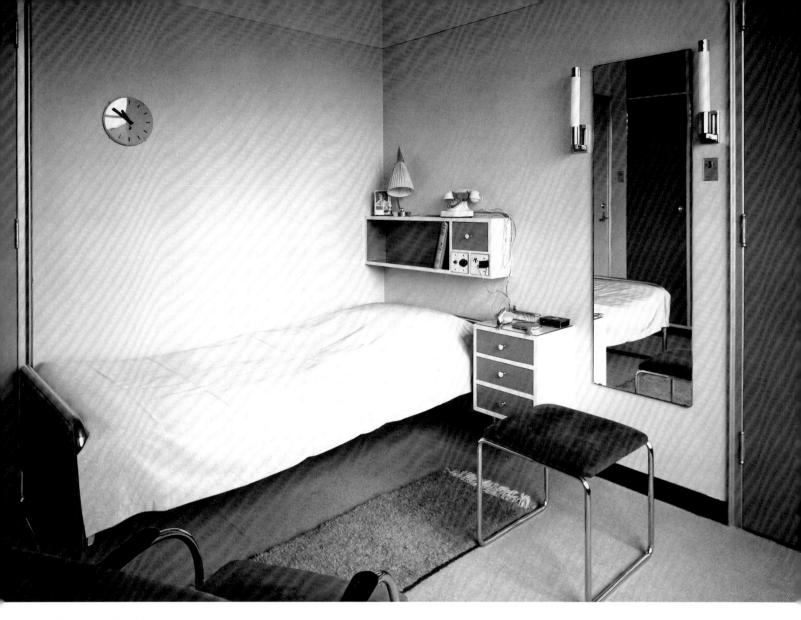

Gé's bedroom with built-in radio,
1933

three sides by space and glass. Directly facing the door was the grand piano, with a sofa on the right. Further to the right was Mrs Sonneveld's writing desk, with a view of the lawn, and behind the partition was the library containing Mr Sonneveld's desk and chairs beside the open hearth. The window strip ran across the entire width of the house, some 17 unbroken metres of glass in total. To the left of the grand piano was the veranda adjoining the dining room, which could be closed off from the living room by a curtain. In old-fashioned terms this enormous living room is a combination of salon, music room, veranda, dining room, boudoir and smoking room. The functions of sitting and receiving guests, making music and listening to it, sitting outside, eating, writing and reading[32] were usually allocated to separate rooms. However, exactly as Nieuwe Bouwen prescribed, they are here combined to produce a greater sense of space. The experience of outdoors, either on the roofed veranda or through the panoramic view of the former Land van Hoboken, contributed significantly to that sense of space. The view of the vast lawn from the house was only one side of the motto 'see and be seen'. The presence of so much glass meant that passers-by could literally observe what was going on in the house, but metaphorically too anyone who was interested could look over the family's shoulder into the house. The living room was only open to friends, acquaintances, relatives and business relations, but soon after the completion of the house it acquired much wider fame through its inclusion in various publications. The most important of these was the home magazine *Het Landhuis* [The country house], which published a whole series of interior photographs by Piet Zwart in February 1934.[33] Moreover, a photograph of the sitting

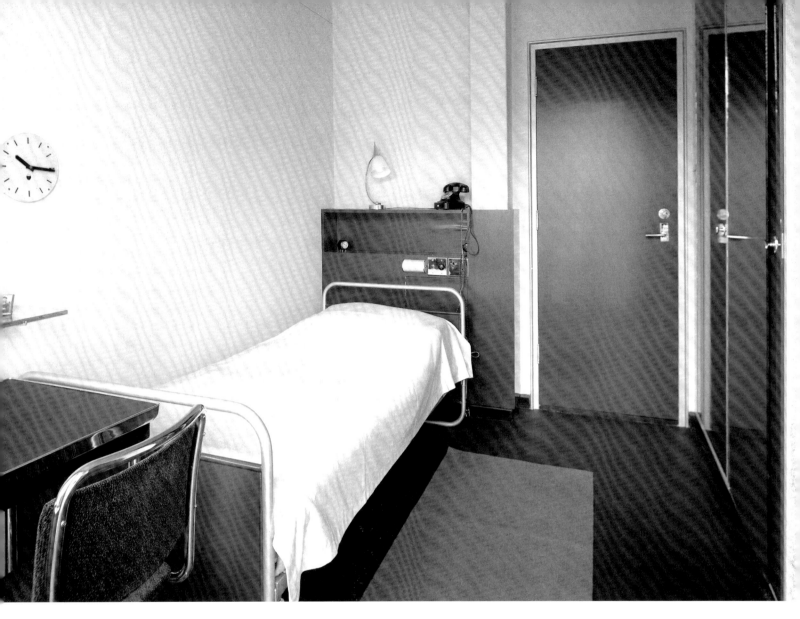

The bedroom of one of the servants
with built-in radio and call-bell
system, 1933

room, taken by Jan Kamman, was released for use in the product catalogue of the Gispen company (furniture catalogue no. 52, 1934). The interior of The Sonneveld House thus came to serve as the model for the interior of an upper-middle-class home with steel furniture and Giso lamps. In addition, the usual project discussions of the building appeared in trade magazines, including Bouwkundig Weekblad [Architectural Weekly], as was common practice for important designs by

architects. The location on the edge of the former Land van Hoboken, which was redesigned as the Museumpark in 1933, made the house familiar to many Rotterdammers. They went to the Westzeedijk on Sundays to go for a stroll and to watch the boats. The Heuvel was a place to drink lemonade in the summer and to go tobogganing in the winter. The new Museum Boijmans attracted a flood of culturally interested visitors from Rotterdam and further afield.

32 The whole family was addicted to reading. Mrs Sonneveld and the daughters are often represented reading, but Mr Sonneveld owned an extensive library too. About half of the family's book collection is still in the hands of the family. A part of it has been replaced in the house in the Jongkindstraat.

33 Most of the contemporary photographs were taken by the photographers Jan Kamman and Piet Zwart. Jan Kamman concentrated on

the exterior. Piet Zwart, who had a reputation as a designer as well as photographer, probably photographed the interior of the house as early as August 1933. This was not by chance: Piet Zwart worked at the time for Bruynzeel, the factory that had supplied the beautiful flat wooden doors for the house and the parquet floor in the studio. The negative numbers are accompanied by strange comments such as 'two doors' and 'four doors' instead of the expected locations.

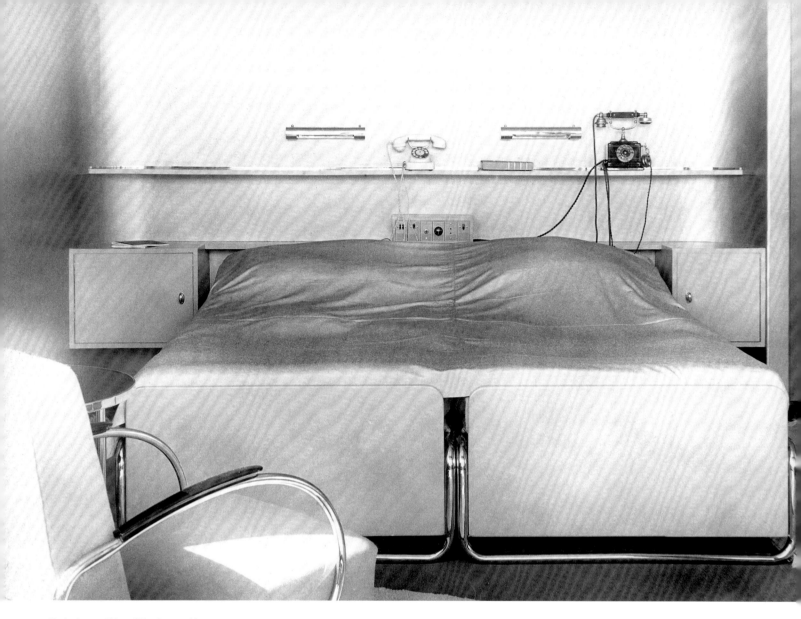

The bedroom of Mr and Mrs Sonneveld,
with built-in radio, call-bell system and
internal and external telephones, 1933

A 'modern' life-style

The principles of Nieuwe Bouwen and Nieuwe Wonen
are often indicated with the motto: 'light, air and space',
but living in large, empty and light rooms also called
for a modern life-style. Given the cult of cleanliness
that prevailed in The Sonneveld Household, living in a
light house will not have raised many problems for
the family. It will have appealed to Mrs Sonneveld in
particular because it was easy to keep clean.[34]

Fresh air and physical well-being have been intrin-
sically linked to one another since the nineteenth
century. The balconies, roof terrace, veranda and
garden contribute to the possibility of intensively using
the outdoor space, and garden photographs show
that they were often put to that use. The Sonneveld
family also had a keen interest in sport. They went on
active holidays in the open air and walked intensively,
especially in the mountains. The hikes were mainly held

in the Alps and in the Black Forest. Mr Sonneveld's
interest in sport can also be seen from the fact that in
1928 he took his eldest daughter to the Olympic
Games in Amsterdam. He was also a swimmer, although
he only received his swimming diploma later in life.
Associates from Van Nelle swam in the Tuinderstraat
swimming pool on Saturday mornings, and a lot of joint
sport went on inside Van Nelle too.[35] Sports fields were
laid out behind the factory especially for the employees. This was the home ground of the Van Nelle team,
the Rising Hope, of which Mr Sonneveld was chairman
for years. Physical activity was recommended because
it was healthy, just like breathing fresh air, taking
proper care of one's body, and hygiene. The sportive
policy of the directors is evident from the various sports
clubs within the company and the reports on their
activities in the factory newsletters.

The bedroom of Mr and Mrs Sonneveld,
looking towards the bathroom, 1933

The new house of the Sonneveld family was large.
The living room was of princely dimensions, and the
proportions of the kitchen and of the parents' bedroom
are striking too. The tubular furniture is part and parcel
of modern architecture – it is disembodied, as it were.
The window strips mean that you can look straight
through the house, and the open character of the
furniture works in a similar way. Besides, the metal
reflects the space and everything around it, enhancing
the impression of transparency and disembodiedness.
The family must have become very attached to the
space and to the tubular furniture, because they never
altered the interior. Moreover, when they moved to
their new home consisting of two apartments made

into one in the City Flat, 140-142 Schiedamsevest, in
1955, they furnished it with the same tubular furniture
and reused some elements from the old house in the
Jongkindstraat, such as the built-in red dining room
cupboard, the electric clocks, and the even lighting
from the ceiling.[36]

The decision to settle in Rotterdam will have been taken
from the very first because they were proud of the city
on the Maas: it was their city, the city of the future.
The choice of the site just west of the old city centre
where they had spent their entire adult life is a natural
consequence of the affinity that they must have felt
with their own neighbourhood. The choice of a new

34 For instance, there were (expensive)
sheets of natural stone under the radiators to
make it easier to mop the floor, and the rubber
floors in the corridors and on the stairs were
regularly scrubbed.

35 *Vereenigingsnieuws* 1 (1925), Rotterdam
Municipal Archive, Archives of the heirs of Widow
J. Van Nelle, inv. no. 952. A.H. Sonneveld was a
familiar figure in the sports association, according
to the *Vereenigingsnieuws* 3 (1927) 1.

36 NAI, BROX Archive 1070.

Studio with the desks of Puck and
Gé and with a view of the stairs
leading to the veranda, 1933

Mr and Mrs Sonneveld with the
latter's brother, Gerard Bos,
in the garden, 1935

The Sonneveld family with guests
in the garden, 1936

house and a new interior will have been easier for them as nouveaux riches than if there had been a family house or family antiques. Besides, the turn towards a modern design was in harmony with their predilection for contemporary art rather than the old masters. Their acquisition of the sculpture by John Rädecker (1885-1956),[37] and of the maritime and river scenes by J.K. Leurs (1865-1938), P.J.C. Gabriël (1828-1903), G. Altmann (1877-1940) and W.B. Tholen (1860-1931) is an obvious sign that the couple liked modern art.[38]

I am not convinced that they both necessarily shared the high expectations of the modernists about a morally better future. The international striving for emancipation arising from the purification of the formal idiom was nothing for them, if only because they were doers rather than thinkers. They stood with both feet firmly planted on the ground. But I do think it likely that from the start they wanted a house that suited them like a bespoke suit. They will have loved the result. The modern house, the new interior, and the consistent harmonisation of all the various elements corresponded to their vision of the manipulable future. At any rate, the house of the Sonneveld family gives the impression of the fulfilment of a long cherished dream of the future.

37 The family owned two works by this sculptor – the lion, and a portrait bust (of the youngest daughter?). The lion remained in the family, the portrait was auctioned at Mak van Waay in 1968.

38 These painters are mentioned in a valuation report from 1988 in the possession of the late Mrs Magdalena Hoefnagel-Sonneveld. Two of these paintings were still in her possession. She also owned T.H. Rousseau's panel *Interior with dog and cat*, which had hung in Mr Sonneveld's library in the Jongkindstraat. According to Lenie, all the paintings were bought by Bertus Sonneveld. Although he did not like abstract art, he liked work by contemporary artists best.

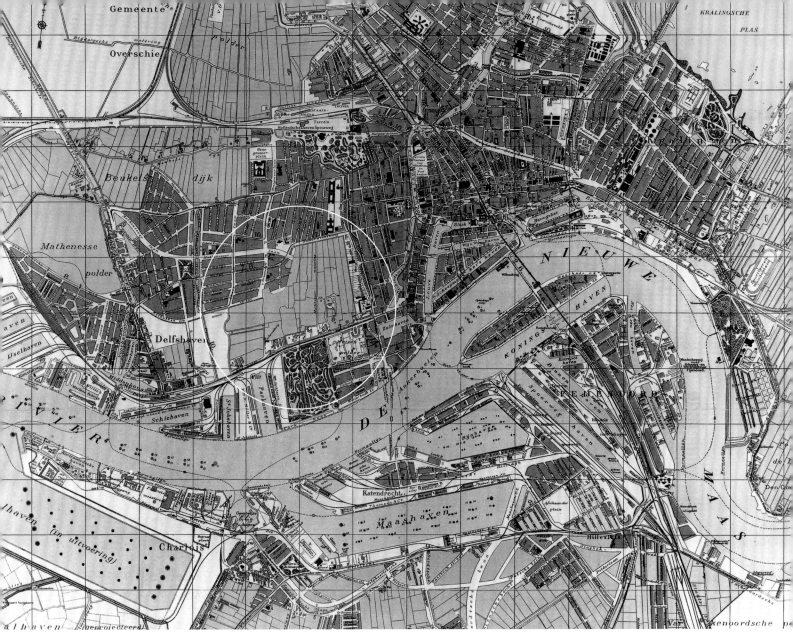

Map of Rotterdam, 1913
The empty area contains the Land
van Hoboken, which was part of
the southern Cool polder

The Dijkzigt Villa Park

Elly Adriaansz

More open buildings (villas) should be made available, for which there is a great demand and by which the better situated can obtain homes in an attractive location, to encourage settling here in the city and to discourage leaving for somewhere else.[1]

Four villas were built in the 1930s in the small Dijkzigt Villa Park in Rotterdam, right in the centre of the city and a stone's throw from Museum Boijmans. One of these villas was The Sonneveld House, named after its first occupant, who commissioned it to be built. Two more villas were added to the group in the 1950s and 1960s.

Villas for wealthy citizens were already a subject of political and private debate in Rotterdam in the nineteenth century, but in the first three decades of the twentieth century attention was focused on a typical Rotterdam phenomenon: the city did not have enough luxury homes for its well-to-do residents, and thus indirectly encouraged their departure to other districts. This issue also attracted the attention of the urban élite in its offensive for the improvement and renewal of the city and its growth to become 'Great Rotterdam' or 'Modern City'.[2] A major cause of the problem lay in

the one-sided orientation of the city council from 1880 onwards on the development of Rotterdam as an international transit port, with the consequence of considerable neglect of the appearance and cultural life of the city.[3]

There are no statistics available on the number of citizens of Rotterdam who left, but there must have been quite a few of them. In this connection the word 'exodus' crops up regularly until the 1930s. Commuting was encouraged by the construction or improvement of public transport links, the rapidly growing use of the car, and the abolition of commuter tax. New ideas about living in a healthy way and an active enjoyment of garden and landscape also played a role. Living outside the city became a way of life for a select group. The Hague and Wassenaar were particularly popular as new residential areas, as well as districts closer to Rotterdam such as Hillegersberg, Overschie and Schiebroek, or Rockanje and Oostvoorne behind the dunes on the island of Voorne in South Holland. The Hague and Wassenaar encouraged luxurious homes by low taxes and offering reasonably priced plots of land in an attractive urban or rural setting. A. Plate, one of the key figures in the socio-cultural élite network of Rotterdam in the 1920s, once commented on the exodus of friends and colleagues that '... nowadays you can't get people together in the evenings any more because they live in Wassenaar'.[4]

Plans for villa parks within the border of Rotterdam can be found between 1900 and the Second World War for Kralingen, in the eastern part of the city – especially Kralingse Bos (1908-1933), Park Rozenburg (1911) and 's-Gravenhof (1926) – and for the southern Cool polder area, popularly known as the Land van Hoboken. This was situated in the western part of the

1 Minutes of the Rotterdam City Council, 20 January 1927.
2 See L.A. de Klerk, *Particuliere plannen. Denkbeelden en initiatieven van de stedelijke elite inzake volkswoningbouw en stedebouw in Rotterdam, 1860-1950*, Rotterdam 1998, esp. the chapter 'City Beautiful in Rotterdam', 185-210.

3 P. van de Laar, *Stad van formaat. Geschiedenis van Rotterdam in de negentiende en twintigste eeuw*, Zwolle 2000, 91-125.
4 See L.A. de Klerk, *Particuliere plannen. Denkbeelden en initiatieven van de stedelijke elite inzake volkswoningbouw en stedebouw in Rotterdam, 1860-1950*, Rotterdam 1998, 41.

Albert Otten, Villa building in Park Rozenbrug, 1922 (bombed) (from: *Moderne Bouwkunst in Nederland. Het Groote Landhuis* 6 (1933) 31)

Villas beside the Groene Wetering (formerly Slotlaan) in 's-Gravenhof, ca. 1935
Villa on the left designed by Dirk Roosenburg (1928)

Granpré Molière, Verhagen and Kok, K.P. van der Mandele House in 's-Gravenhof, 1930 (from: *Moderne Bouwkunst in Nederland. Het Groote Landhuis* 6 (1933) 25)

Eastern part of the Land van Hoboken, ca. 1915. From right to left: the trees of the Dijkzigt estate belonging to the Van Hoboken family, the Roman Catholic St Ignatius Church (episcopal church, demolished in 1968), situated on the southern side of the Westzeedijk, and the Reformed Nieuwe Zuiderkerk with the tower under construction. This was situated on the northern side of the Westzeedijk and was demolished in 1969. To the left of it is the Deaconesses Nursing Home (demolished in 1990), and the trees in the back gardens of the Westersingel.

city, between the present-day Delfshaven and the centre of Rotterdam.[5] Both Kralingen (annexed by Rotterdam in 1895) and the Land van Hoboken were known for their rural atmosphere, estates (sometimes centuries-old) and country houses where the rich citizens of Rotterdam lived permanently or spent the summer. The attractive woods, the construction of landscape parks and gardens on the estates, and the peaceful atmosphere were what private and local government administrators regarded as the ideal setting for villas.

The Dijkzigt Villa Park / Land of Hoboken
The Dijkzigt Villa Park in the Museumpark in the centre of Rotterdam is part of the Dijkzigt urban development plan drawn up by W.G. Witteveen in 1927.

The villas are built on a former estate, the Land of Hoboken, that formed a part of the southern Cool polder.[6] It had been in the possession of the Rotterdam Van Hoboken family since 1850. Van Hoboken was the owner of a shipping company and a distillery, was active in the world of banking and in commodity trade extending to the Far East, and especially the Dutch

East Indies. In the last quarter of the nineteenth century the estate belonged to the brothers Jacobus and Anthony van Hoboken (the latter adopted the name Van Hoboken van Cortgene). The total dimensions of the estate were enormous: 56 hectares, 51 of which were earmarked as meadow. The remaining five hectares comprised the Dijkzigt estate, where Anthony van Hoboken van Cortgene lived in Villa Dijkzigt, surrounded by a park in the style of an English landscape with a lake and an ornamental garden. The estate was bounded on the south by the Westzeedijk, on the north by the Nieuwe Binnenweg, and on the east by the back gardens of the houses on the Westersingel. The western side of the estate was situated to a large extent on the territory of Delfshaven, which was annexed by Rotterdam in 1886. The Westzeedijk contained the entrance to the Dijkzigt estate and a large number of larger and smaller estates, villas, farms, and a few streets of council housing, known as Stroodorp. Some of the buildings belonged to the local authority, which owned about six hectares of land in the southern Cool polder. Because of its central location in the city

J.F. Metzelaar, Villa Dijkzigt (1856), home of the Van Hoboken family, 1927 (from: W. G. Witteveen, *Het uitbreidingsplan voor het Land van Hoboken*, Haarlem 1927, 10)

J. Verheul Dzn., Stable near Villa Dijkzigt, 1881-1882 (completed) (from: *Bouwkundig Weekblad* 2 (1882) 10)

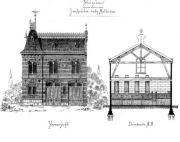

Villa Groendal (1873) was on the northern side of the Westzeedijk on the Land van Hoboken, 1906. In 1902 the villa became the property of the local authority, which made it available to the Montefiori Association, an organisation that helped Jewish immigrants.

Villa Schooneberg, ca.1920. The grounds fulfilled a variety of functions from the nineteenth century on.

and the refusal of the Van Hoboken family to sell the land, the Land van Hoboken was already an obstacle to attempts by the local authority to expand in the nineteenth century. Compulsory purchase proved to be impossible because of the economic importance of the Van Hobokens for Rotterdam; they had informed the city council that they would leave the city and take all their companies with them in the event of compulsory purchase. L.J.C.J. van Ravesteyn, solicitor and historian of the city of Rotterdam, described the Land van Hoboken as a rural idyll and as '... one of the most remarkable things in this growing and bustling city, the land where, separated by only a ditch from one of the busiest main roads, the cattle grazed in tranquillity

and the heron patiently waited for his prey beside the ditch'.[7]

In 1906 the Van Hoboken family sold a small strip of land to the local authority to widen the Nieuwe Binnenweg. After the death of Jacobus van Hoboken in 1916, a serious attempt was made by the heirs to sell 30 hectares of land. The buyer was a private combination, consisting of a number of prominent citizens of Rotterdam. The sale was thwarted by a legal action instigated by Anthony van Hoboken van Cortgene, who demanded separation and division of the land and recognition as tenant and manager of part of the grounds. Apart from a few plots, Van Hoboken van Cortgene bought the disputed land from the heirs, thereby becoming owner

5 The building of villas in Hillegersberg, Overschie and Schiebroek is not mentioned here because these local authorities only became a part of Rotterdam in 1941.

6 For a detailed history of the Land van

Hoboken and the six villas see: *Wiederhall* 20 (2001), 'Rotterdam Museumpark Villa's'.

7 L.J.C.J. van Ravesteyn, *Rotterdam in de twintigste eeuw. De ontwikkeling van de stad vóór 1940*, Rotterdam 1948, 208.

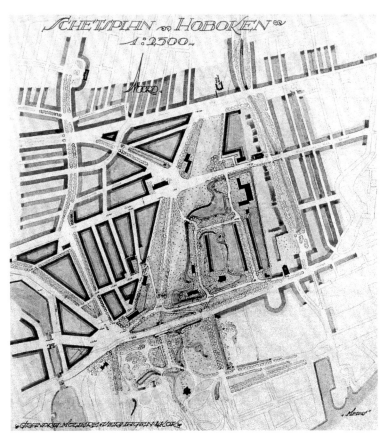

Granpré Molière, Verhagen and Kok,
Plan for the Land van Hoboken,
'Vereeniging voor Stadsverbetering
Nieuw Rotterdam', 1923

W.G. Witteveen, Dijkzigt Extension
Plan, 1927

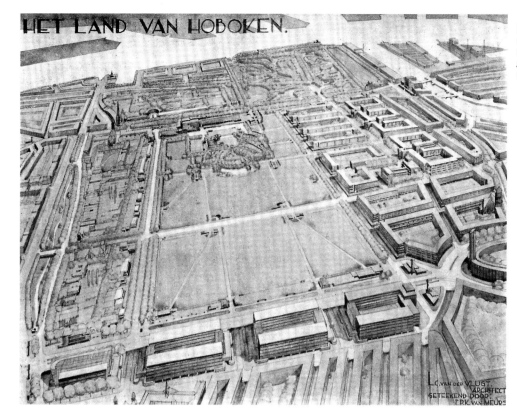

HET LAND VAN HOBOKEN.

L.C. van der Vlugt. Plan for the Land van Hoboken, 1925 (from: *Bouwen, tijdschrift voor Holland en Indië gewijd aan de belangen van het bouwvak* 3 (1925) 1, 3)

of the whole Land van Hoboken. This guaranteed his main wish – no exploitation and undisturbed calm.[8]

Nevertheless, the long period of the status quo between the Van Hoboken family and the local authority did not stop the preparation of various plans for expansion on this large area of land. The plans of 1883 and 1887 which were made for the southern Cool polder by G.J. de Jongh, director of the municipal public works department from 1879 to 1910, focused on the construction of the port, and particularly on his plan to link the Schie with the Maas. He did not express an opinion on villa construction. However, in his 1897 plan, part of the Cool polder was to become a prominent residential town with a new representative city centre and a spacious residential quarter. This Quartier Léopold, as he called it, consisted of mixed luxury and working-class housing, railway lines and boulevards.[9] As the initiator of the major dockside works in Rotterdam, De Jongh pointed out that the expansion of a commercial city was a fundamentally different matter from that of a luxury city like The Hague. 'While it is important there to make a good choice in the construction of main roads, alternating here and there with a square or a small park, to attract residents and outsiders to settle

there, in the case of the expansion of Rotterdam it is important to bear in mind that people do not usually come here to spend the money that they have earned elsewhere, but that they come here to earn it, so that the conditions for doing so have to be taken into account in the expansion. And those conditions are to be found in a trading city: bring water so that ships can come, make rail links.'[10]

Villas are first mentioned in the 1917 expansion plan drawn up by A.C. Burgdorffer, who succeeded De Jongh as director of the municipal public works department.[11] In view of the special characteristics of the Land van Hoboken, it was given a single function: that of a prominent and tranquil residential district for the wealthiest citizens of Rotterdam. This classicistic cross-shaped plan envisages an elongated strip of water closed off by a monumental building. The closed development alternates with a variety of villas within a strict boulevard system. Burgdorffer left the former Dijkzigt estate intact. The plan was ratified by the Rotterdam city council in 1920.

During the test of strength between the local authority and the heirs of the Van Hoboken family after the death of Anthony van Hoboken van Cortgene in 1922,

8   The sale concerned the western part of the Land van Hoboken, including the Melkkop tea-house and the tennis courts there. Van Hoboken van Cortgene bought the remaining thirty hectares for two million guilders. Van Vollenhoven press cuttings 10-31 December 1916; 25 January-15 February 1917, and 21 October-14 November 1917.

9   L.J.C.J. van Ravesteyn, *Rotterdam in de twintigste eeuw. De ontwikkeling van de stad vóór 1940*, Rotterdam 1948, 174.

10   Collection of the printed documents 1887, 5.

11   Van Ravesteyn claims that this plan was drawn up by Granpré Molière. See L.J.C.J. van Ravesteyn, *Rotterdam in de twintigste eeuw. De ontwikkeling van de stad vóór 1940*, Rotterdam 1948, 207.

Jan van Teeffelen, Villa for Peter Merkes (7 Museumpark), 1932-1934, photograph from 1945. The villa had a roof terrace and a stone pergola enclosed with glass in the garden. In the 1960s the outside walls and the interior were drastically modified and the original brick wall was plastered.

G. Baas and L. Stokla, Villa for C.H. Kraaijeveld (11 Museumpark), 1938-1939, photograph from 1967

the estate passed for a time into the hands of a private working company, N.V. Dijkzigt, formed by the heirs. The Van Dam-Schaap plan, which was commissioned by the company, to turn the Land van Hoboken into a working-class district became notorious. The furious Rotterdam community, who regarded the Land van Hoboken as a pearl in the city, immediately christened this plan 'The Black Plan'. The local authority refused to cooperate in any way with its implementation. Granpré Molière referred to a '... building density that outdoes all entrepreneurial cynicism'.[12] Alternative proposals were made by architects and by the 'New Rotterdam' Association for Urban Improvement. The plan drawn up by Granpré Molière, Verhagen and Kok for this association in 1923 envisages a fan-shaped structure with park and lake and a few monumental accents for the central area of the Land van Hoboken, surrounded by continuous buildings. The design anticipates Witteveen's 1927 plan.[13]

In May 1924 the council bought the Land van Hoboken for the sum of four million guilders. At the family's request, the area was given the name Dijkzigt after the sale had been concluded. The Burgdorffer plan soon proved to be impractical. Villa construction was not viable because of the high price of the estate and the poor financial situation of the local authority. There was also a desire to create an urban green belt to link up with the landscape construction of the Westersingel, the Park on the harbour, and the Zoo in the north.

L.C. van der Vlugt's private design for the Land van Hoboken in 1925 seems to be a response to this.

It also takes the growth of road traffic into account. Wide roads intersect the spacious central area with the estate. Closed and open blocks with lawns, meadows and terraces were planned for the northern and western parts. Closed and open development alternate along the road on the eastern side. A monumental building closes it off at the Westzeedijk. Van der Vlugt's design is a demonstration of the functionalist ideas about architecture and urban development of the Modern Movement.

In 1927 the Rotterdam local authority accepted the Dijkzigt expansion plan by W.G. Witteveen, city architect and director of the Urban Development Department that had been set up in the previous year.[14] Almost immediately the council started regular and compulsory purchase procedures to obtain all of the land and buildings on the Land van Hoboken. The total demolition of the villas, the historic estates, the Stroodorp and other buildings on the southern border of the former estate, with the exception of Villa Dijkzigt, followed in the same year.

The Dijkzigt Plan consisted of a wide, fan-shaped landscape zone that formed the desired link with the existing canal and parks. The spatial organisation of the green central area – called Museumpark by a council decision in 1929 – was brought about using varied landscape elements. Seen from the Nieuwe Binnenweg, this comprised an open area (entrance), a lake and trees that effected the transition to the woods of the former Dijkzigt estate. Witteveen planned a museum, an ornamental garden with ponds, a children's

L.C. van der Vlugt, Villa for
H.J. Boevé (9 Museumpark),
1932-1933

playground and an open air theatre for the eastern part of the site. The area to the north and west of this was to be built up with blocks of buildings, which he considered to fit in well with the massive quality of the city. The plan also envisaged several monumental buildings: a large office, a grammar school, an electricity company, 'a Dutch skyscraper', and a museum – science and modern technology were united.

Witteveen considered that there was no place for open development – which had formed a part of Burgdorffer's 1917 plan and had become a matter for debate again in connection with Witteveen's plan – 'because the land earmarked for building is not deep enough to form a harmonious transition from this open development to the more massive form of the existing city'.[15] Personal intervention by the councillor for corporation works, A. de Jong, led to a political compromise. The trapezium-shaped area opposite the site of the future museum, that was bounded by Mathenesserlaan, Jongkindstraat and Nieuwe Binnenweg, was allocated for the construction of villas. Besides the familiar argument that villas were necessary to make the wealthy citizens stay, De Jong may also have been sensitive to the local authority's criticism of the block that Witteveen had planned for this plot of land because it would obstruct the view of the museum from the city. The initial keenness of buyers for plots of land on Dijkzigt fell sharply as a result of the international economic crisis of the early 1930s and the council's slow handling of purchase requests. The council's dithering was connected with the construction of the Maas Tunnel; it did not want to make a firm decision yet because it was still unclear how traffic from the tunnel to the city would be handled. In the end, five candidates were left over from the twelve potential buyers. Consequently, the council's plan for a series of villas and residences was reduced to the building of a few detached villas. The council also went back on its intention of having the villas designed by the Brinkman & Van der Vlugt firm of architects. A clause to this effect had originally been included in the provisional deeds because four candidates had chosen Van der Vlugt as architect. The price of the land fluctuated between 22.20 and 33.30 guilders per square metre (the equivalent of between 160 and 240 euros today).

The various council departments turned a deaf ear to complaints from their electors about these low prices. Their priority was luxury housing, whatever the price, as is shown by their advice to the councillor: 'We emphatically do not recommend raising the prices, especially as we know that several candidates own property in other local authorities and increasing the prices will result in their departure from the district'.[16] The planning permission regulations were strict: sale only became definitive after the council had approved the façades of the villas.

12   M.J. Granpré Molière, 'Het Land Hoboken', *Tijdschrift voor Volkshuisvesting en Stedebouw*, 30 (1922), 187.

13   In 1923 this association also submitted a plan by the Meischke and Schmidt firm of architects to the local authority. L.H.E. van Hylckama Vlieg also reacted to 'The Black Plan' with a design in the *Bouwkundig Weekblad*. See: *Bouwkundig Weekblad*, 44 (1923) 19, 207-209.

14   Minutes of the Rotterdam City Council, 29 January 1927.

15   W.G. Witteveen, *Het uitbreidingsplan voor het Land van Hoboken*, Haarlem 1927, 24.

16   Corporation Works, dossier 2528, 1930.

The firm of Brinkman & Van der Vlugt built two very modern villas between 1932 and 1933: one for the doctor H.J. Boevé, the other for A.H. (Albert) Sonneveld, one of the directors of the Van Nelle factory. The villa of the well-known Rotterdam jeweller Peter Merkes, designed by Jan van Teeffelen, was constructed between 1932 and 1934. The block-shaped, luxury building was constructed in brick and designed as a temple for Merkes's art collection. The last of the prewar villas on Dijkzigt dates from 1938-1939. It was designed by the architects Gerrit Baas and Leonard Stokla for J.C. Kraaijeveld, one of the directors of the Adriaan Volker dredging company in Sliedrecht. After the war the doctor P. Van der Meer commissioned the architect Harry Kammer to build a sober villa in a functionalist style (1957-1958). Finally, the last villa on Dijkzigt was built between 1960 and 1961. It was commissioned by the doctor J.H. ten Kate from the architect F. (Ernest) Groosman.[17]

The Dijkzigt Villa Park was constructed on the historic land of a former estate, an area that had once been a part of the meadows of the Land van Hoboken, and in this new situation fell within the direct cultural sphere of influence of Museum Boijmans. The magisterial view of the spacious Museumpark was destroyed for the occupants in the Jongkindstraat at the corner of the Mathenesserlaan in 1940 when the bombing of Rotterdam was followed by the building of a complex of emergency shops on the site of the Museumpark. These were demolished in the 1950s after the completion of the Lijnbaan shopping centre and the breakthrough of the Westblaak. The gradual filling up of the park started about ten years later with the construction of the Dijkzigt Hospital and Medical Faculty (1965-1968), the Netherlands Architecture Institute (1988-1993), and the Sophia Children's Hospital (1987-1994). The vision of a long park with its depth perspective which had formed the core of Witteveen's Dijkzigt Plan was gone for ever.

17   Addresses: villa Peter Merkes (7 Museumpark), H.J. Boevé (9 Museumpark), Albert (A.H.) Sonneveld (12 Jongkindstraat), C.H. Kraaijeveld (11 Museumpark), P. van der Meer (16 Jongkindstraat) and J.H. ten Kate (18 Jongkindstraat). See also: *Wiederhall* 20 (2001), 'Rotterdam Museumpark Villa's'.

Dijkzigt Villa Park, 1940, with smoke
from the bombing of Rotterdam in
the background.

View of Museumpark under construction from the roof terrace of the Sonneveld House; in the distance the Margarine Unie factory (now Rotterdam Polytechnic), ca. 1935

The Museumpark under construction with a view of Museum Boijmans, with House Boevé in front, seen from the outdoor room of the Sonneveld House, ca. 1935

The Museumpark under construction, seen from the roof terrace of the Sonneveld House, with a view of the Nieuwe Binnenweg, ca. 1935

The Sonneveld House

The design history within the oeuvre of Brinkman and Van der Vlugt and in relation to contemporaries

Joris Molenaar

Situation of Dijkzigt

The large open area of the former Land van Hoboken that was situated in the centre of Rotterdam was transformed in accordance with the Dijkzigt Plan in the early 1930s into a park landscape centred on the luxuriant groves of the former estate and surrounded by new buildings.[1] According to this plan, behind the Westersingel the Jongkindstraat came to run between the Nieuwe Binnenweg and the extended Mathenesserlaan. On the western side of the street lay the open area of the Museumpark, that ran into the Maaspark on the other side of the Westzeedijk, while on the eastern side a plot of land was made ready for the construction of villas. Between 1929 and 1931 twelve candidates from the well-to-do bourgeoisie applied to the city council for permission to buy a plot of land to build a luxury residence or villa on. However, they were kept waiting for years before the council had made the land allocation and proceeded to sell plots of land. That is why only three villas were actually under construction in 1932: a brick villa opposite Museum Boijmans designed for P. Merkes, a Rotterdam jeweller, by the architect J.F. van Teeffelen, and two modern white villas designed by the firm of Brinkman and Van der Vlugt. The smaller of these is on the left, next to the Merkes villa, and was designed for H.J. Boevé, a paediatric surgeon; the other is the substantial villa at no. 12 Jongkindstraat that was built for A.H. Sonneveld, a member of the board of directors of the Van Nelle company.[2] The design and the construction of the villa must have been a far-reaching and adventurous process of modernisation for this family. The two-and-a half-year planning period that preceded the actual building work can be followed on the basis of the design stages, although the considerations of the client and the architects can only be deduced from indirect sources. Starting out from the information that has been obtained on the family and on the plans for Dijkzigt, a close reading of the drawings enables us to follow the design process chronologically.

The Sonneveld family and its relation to the Van Nelle company

Albertus (Bertus) Hendrikus Sonneveld moved to Rotterdam as a young man in 1900 to enter the employ of Van Nelle.[3] In 1912 he married Gesine Grietje Bos. The couple had two daughters, Magda (Puck) and Gesine (Gé). Sonneveld was given a position of great responsibility as a tobacco buyer at an early stage in his career. To that end he spent a few months each year abroad, mainly in the United States. During his stay there In 1912 he received a visit from the eldest son of one of the owners of Van Nelle, C.H. (Kees) van der Leeuw (1890-1973).[4] He was looking into the tobacco side of the Van Nelle company with a view to his entry into the company in 1913. The personal contact between Sonneveld and Kees van der Leeuw dates from this period. In 1917 Kees van der Leeuw joined the board of directors of the Van Nelle family concern. This enabled him to dedicate himself to his passion – improving the working conditions of the factory workers by the development and implementation of new building plans for Van Nelle. In 1919 Sonneveld was promoted to become a deputy manager of Van Nelle, which also entitled him to the bonus scheme which benefitted the Van Nelle management. As a result, the Sonneveld family was able to climb up into the circles of the well-to-do Rotterdam bourgeoisie with a leading position in the world of industry.

1 On the history of the Land van Hoboken see also: Elly Adriaansz, 'History. A modern residential neighbourhood in the city', in: *Wiederhall* 20 (2001), 'Museumpark Rotterdam'.

2 This chapter is based on the research results of the study: *De architectuur van Brinkman and Van der Vlugt esthetisch beschouwd, 1e fase de villa's*, carried out by the author between 1995 and 1997 for the De Stenen Tafel Foundation in Rotterdam, with financial support from the Architecture Promotion Fund and the Netherlands Foundation for Fine Arts, Design and Architecture in Amsterdam. On the plans of Brinkman and Van der Vlugt in Dijkzigt see also: Joris Molenaar, 'Visions of Dijkzigt, Brinkman and Van der Vlugt', in: *Wiederhall* 20 (2001), 'Museumpark Rotterdam'. An earlier publication by the author on The Sonneveld House is: Joris Molenaar, 'Beyond an arid functionalism. The Sonneveld House by Brinkman and Van der Vlugt (1929-1933)', in: *Archis* 8 (1993), 53-63. The insights of that article have been partly revised on the basis of later study and experiences during the restoration of the house.

3 The information about the company 'De Erven de Wed. J. van Nelle' and the connections of the persons named with Van Nelle are based on data from the Historical Archive of De Ervan de Wed. J. van Nelle N.V. and the publication: H.F.W. Bantje, *Twee eeuwen met de weduwe. Geschiedenis van De Erven de Wed. J. van Nelle N.V. 1782-1982*, Rotterdam 1981.

4 See: correspondence of J.J. van der Leeuw to C.H. van der Leeuw 1912, Historical Archive of De Ervan de Wed. J. van Nelle.

Members of the board of directors of Van Nelle on the raised site on which the Van Nelle factory in Overschie was to be built, from left to right: M. de Bruyn, C.H. van der Leeuw, A.H. Sonneveld and A.H.J. Cauters, spring 1925

Brinkman and Van der Vlugt, Van Nelle factory complex, Overschie, end 1929

L.C. van der Vlugt and J.G. Wiebenga, School of Technology and Industry in Groningen, 1922

Brinkman and Van der Vlugt, Van der Leeuw House, Kralingse Plaslaan, Rotterdam, 1928-1930

The economic growth of Van Nelle took a strong upward turn in the 1920s. The company was therefore able to build the hypermodern factory complex in Overschie between 1925 and 1931. Kees van der Leeuw had been calling for this for years, and the J.A. Brinkman and L.C. van der Vlugt firm of architects in Rotterdam started to make the first building plans in 1925.[5] At first Michiel Brinkman (1873-1925) was the architect for Van Nelle, but he died suddenly in the spring of 1925. L.C. (Leen) van der Vlugt (1894-1936) had been established as an independent architect in Rotterdam for more than five years by this time, and had achieved something of a reputation for the School of Technology and Industry that he had designed with Jan Gerko Wiebenga in Groningen in 1922. Kees van der Leeuw must also have been familiar with his private plan for the Land of Hoboken. When the Brinkman family with the young J.A. (Jan) Brinkman as heir (he was still a student at the time) pleaded to retain the assignment for Van Nelle, Van der Leeuw laid down the condition that he would choose an architect for the factory building who would work together with Brinkman. The choice fell on Leen van der Vlugt. After the building of the Van Nelle factory, the members of the Van der Leeuw manufacturing family had their own homes modernised or new ones built by the same team of architects. The cultural and technological innovations of the time, especially in France, Germany, England and the United States, influenced the taste of this well-to-do élite. The many business trips that they made, not only in Europe and the United States but also to South America, Africa and the Dutch East Indies, familiarised them with the comfort of luxury liners, Pullman carriages and the American Grand Hotels. Kees van der Leeuw also took a keen interest in the latest developments in the field of factory construction.[6] Besides the great importance that he attached to good and healthy

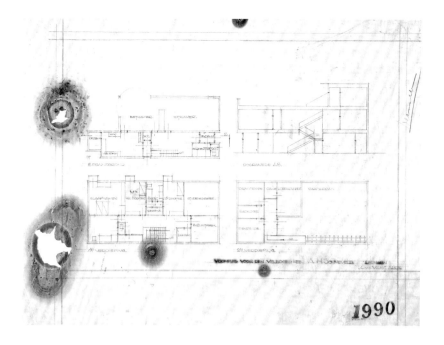

Sonneveld House, first sketch
proposal no. 1990, ca. end 1929

1990

conditions for the staff, with the right facilities for light, air and spatial conditions, he was also very interested in modern architecture and art. He therefore felt it to be his personal responsibility to pay full attention to the non-quantifiable aspects of the construction.[7] The building of the Van Nelle factory in Overschie between 1925 and 1931 and the construction and total interior design of the house designed for him in the Kralingse Plaslaan in Rotterdam between 1928 and 1930 by Brinkman and Van der Vlugt are the best-known examples of his enlightened patronage. The latter private assignment inspired two members of the board and later directors of the Van Nelle factory, Mathijs de Bruyn (1881-1963) and Albert Sonneveld, to commission this firm of architects to design new, detached homes for their families in 1929. The villa for the De Bruyn family was built between 1930 and 1931 in Schiedam. The Sonneveld family had to wait until 1933 before their city residence in the Dijkzigt Plan was completed and furnished.[8]

The Brinkman and Van der Vlugt firm of architects and the first draft proposal for The Sonneveld House

The commissions to built villas in Dijkzigt came for the Brinkman and Van der Vlugt firm of architects at a very welcome moment. At the time of the onset of the international economic crisis of 1929 they still had a well-filled portfolio of assignments, but the building of the new Van Nelle factory in Overschie was already at an advanced stage, the factory was already in use, and only the workshops and the distribution centre beside the Schie were still under construction. Brinkman and Van der Vlugt had received a number of big industrial commissions in 1929 and early 1930 from the circle of Rotterdam industrialists for whom Michiel Brinkman had worked. In 1929 they started on a series of successive assignments: a project for a large silo for the Grain Elevator Company and an extension of the 'De Maas' steam milling factory, both in the Maashaven in Rotterdam; a factory for the Ardath Tobacco Company in Dordrecht; and an extension of the Niehuis and Van den Berg wharf in Delfshaven. We may conclude from this that, with the building for Van Nelle, Brinkman and Van der Vlugt had succeeded in establishing a reputation in Rotterdam as a specialist firm in the field of industrial utilitarian buildings. The knowledge,

5   On the history of the building of the Van Nelle factories see: Joris Molenaar, 'The Van Nelle Factory. Dutch Avantgarde and American Inspiration', in: *Il Modo di Costruire. Atti del I Seminario Internazionale*, Roma 1990, 345-364; and Joris Molenaar, 'Van Nelle's New Factories, American Inspiration and Cooperation', in: *Wiederhall* 14 (1993), 7-17.

6   For this purpose he went on study trips to Germany and elsewhere. He established contact with Walter Gropius during one of these trips. He also went on a very long trip to the factories in the United States in 1926. The report and the documentation on this trip have been partly preserved. Besides the library on architecture that Kees van der Leeuw built up, he and his brother

Dick visited de luxe furniture and interior businesses in Paris, for instance, for inspiration regarding their own interiors. They passed their impressions on to Van der Vlugt.

7   See: C.H. van der Leeuw, *Bouw eener Nieuwe Fabriek. Factoren bij de keuze van terreinen en fabriekstype*, Nederlandsch Instituut voor Efficiency, November 1930.

8   For a detailed account of the history of the Dijkzigt Plan see: Elly Adriaansz, 'History. A modern residential neighbourhood in the city', and for the designs that Brinkman and Van der Vlugt made within the Dijkzigt Plan see: Joris Molenaar, 'Visions of Dijkzigt, Brinkman and Van der Vlugt', both in: *Wiederhall* 20 (2001), 'Museumpark villa's'.

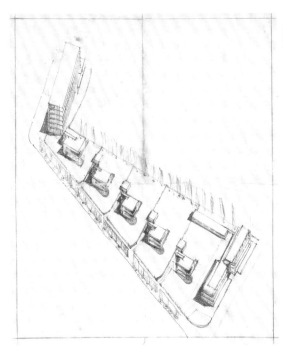

Brinkman and Van der Vlugt,
bird's-eye view sketch of Dijkzigt
Villa Park, January 1931

experience and capacity that had been built up for
Van Nelle could be deployed for all these new commissions. However, when the world crisis showed no signs
of diminishing, the assignments placed with them to
construct new buildings dwindled in 1930 to a mere
two office buildings: one for the branch of the Mees
bank on the 's-Gravendijkwal in Rotterdam, and one
for the Van Stolk Wood Company, opposite Van Nelle
on the Schie. There was thus a lot at stake for the
architects in obtaining the prestigious assignments
in Dijkzigt. In fact, they were already involved from
December 1928 onwards in plans for a new building
for the Volksuniversiteit [Adult Education Centre] in the
Dijkzigt Plan.[9]

There is no situation indicated on the sketch proposal no. 1990 where the name A.H. Sonneveld appears
for the first time. It was done around the autumn of
1929. The floor plan is based on the type of classic
residence like the house at no. 158 Heemraadssingel
where the Sonneveld family was then living, with a
narrow bay for the entrance, a hall leading to the
staircase and kitchen, and beside it a wide bay for the
two rooms separated by a partition, the optional intermediate room, and the conservatory. On the first floor
there are two small rooms behind and in front of the
staircase in the narrow bay, while the wide bay contains
a front and a back room and intermediate rooms. The
conservatory is replaced by a veranda, and instead
of an attic there is a roof construction with servants'
quarters and a guest room beside a roof terrace.

Other interested buyers and the attitude of
the city council

Sonneveld wrote to the Rotterdam City Council on
8 February 1929 to apply for a plot of land on which to
build a villa in the Dijkzigt Plan. Apart from a request
for information about the sale of land made by the

architect Van Teeffelen on behalf of P. Merkes in March
1928, Sonneveld was the first to apply in writing for a
plot of land. Nine months later he had still not received
an official reply from the authorities.[10]

James Catz, another interested candidate who
submitted a similar application to the Rotterdam City
Council on 7 November 1929, contacted Brinkman
and Van der Vlugt the very next day to make a sketch
plan for him.[11] This seems to have prompted them to
start sketching proposals for Sonneveld too. Catz,
however, soon decided not to build a villa at Dijkzigt,
while Sonneveld was kept waiting for clearer information about the land allocation. In the course of 1929
Sonneveld, Merkes and Catz were followed by other
wealthy private individuals who applied for land to build
villas in Dijkzigt. The local government officers involved
advised the city council not to delay any longer but
to proceed to sell plots of land for the building of villas.
However, the attention of the council was drawn to
larger projects, such as the building of a tunnel, a
secondary school, and a brief investigation of the possibility of a concert hall at Dijkzigt, for which Brinkman
and Van der Vlugt carried out studies.

Second sketch design: similarities to
The De Bruyn House

A sketch by Van der Vlugt dated 9 January 1930
(though this must be a mistake for 9 January 1931,
understandable enough at the beginning of a new year)
indicates the villa lots in the urban development con-
text of the sketch proposal for a concert hall and the
office for the Margarine Union (later Unilever): two
buildings whose walls flank the Rochussenstraat and
the Mathenesserlaan, with graduated plots for detached
houses in between. Van der Vlugt tried to adhere to
this principle in his building proposals, as is clearly
indicated on a bird's-eye sketch from around the time

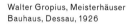
BEGANE GROND.

1E VERDIEPING

2E VERDIEPING

Brinkman and Van der Vlugt, De Bruyn
House, 14 Ary Prinslaan, Schiedam,
ca. 1931

Brinkman and Van der Vlugt,
De Bruyn House, 14 Ary Prinslaan,
Schiedam, (1929-1931)
Floor plans

Walter Gropius, Meisterhäuser
Bauhaus, Dessau, 1926

of the New Year in 1931. The Sonneveld family will have been aware of this idea.

The second sketch design, no. 3294-3297, dates from around that New Year, so it must be based on this allotment of plots of land for four or five detached houses in the Jongkindstraat. This sketch design is worked out in much more detail than the first one, and contains a programme that corresponds to the villa that was actually built, except that the garage is not shown on it (it was probably intended to stand on its own in the garden). The family seem to have devoted some thought in the meantime as to how they wanted to live in the new house, so that the architects could make a detailed plan, including a programme for fixed and movable furniture. The situation of the living area and the kitchen is on the ground floor, and there is a cellar for storage and stocks underneath half of the house. The bedrooms are on the first floor, while the servants and guests had their rooms on the second floor next to a roof terrace. The principle of a residence from the first sketch plan was here replaced by that of a villa with a central hall, which is continued via the staircase up to the top floor. This is similar to the structure of the design for the De Bruyn villa that was built in Schiedam. Construction of that house began in the autumn of 1930, and the Sonneveld family will certainly have been well informed about how the family of Mathijs de Bruyn, a member of the board of Van Nelle like Sonneveld, intended to live! There are also parallels with the Meisterhäuser designed by Walter Gropius near the Bauhaus in Dessau from 1925-1926, particularly the cubic composition and the arrangement of the living room floor with a veranda.

Complications involving parcelling out and the sale of land

After January 1931 consultation took place on the parcelling out of the villa site, both internally within the civil service and externally between Urban Development and potential candidates. This can be seen from the allocation of plots sketched on 25 April 1931, probably by Urban Development, that was sent to the candidates. Brinkman and Van der Vlugt then sketched alternatives for plots of land for detached houses combined with blocks of rows of residences, at right angles to the Mathenesserlaan. This was necessary because the council's proposal hardly took into account the fact that the programmes and budgets of the different candidates varied considerably.

On 6 June 1931 Brinkman and Van der Vlugt received a letter from Urban Development in which plots were proposed to suit the wishes of the remaining candidates. The row of buildings in the Mathenesserlaan opposite Museum Boijmans was changed into a double house with large gardens. In addition, a series of three residences could be built in the Jongkindstraat at the corner of the Mathenesserlaan for candidates with a smaller purse who wanted less land. Further up the Jongkindstraat three large plots were reserved for three detached houses. The graduated parcels as proposed by Van der Vlugt were incorporated in the proposal. The block of buildings in the Rochussenstraat was maintained. On 26 June this plan was incorporated in a memorandum on the sale of land, including the draft offers of land, followed by the final offers of land on 24 July to seven candidates who were considered serious enough and who had had the patience to wait:

9 See: Joris Molenaar, 'Visions of Dijkzigt, Brinkman and Van der Vlugt', in: *Wiederhall* 20 (2001), 'Museumpark villa's'.

10 See: Rotterdam Municipal Archive, Archive of Local Works PW 1930 – 470-7a.

11 Proposal no. 1990 must have been produced at the same time as the sketches that

Brinkman and Van der Vlugt made for the house of James Catz in the period 7 November 1929 - 15 January 1930, because a sketch design no. 1987 dated 20 November 1929 is known for the Catz house for the northernmost plot in the Jongkindstraat.

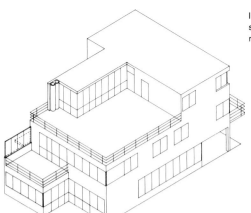

Isometric projection,
sketch proposal no. 3294-3297,
reconstruction Molenaar & Van Winden

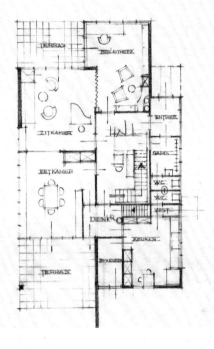

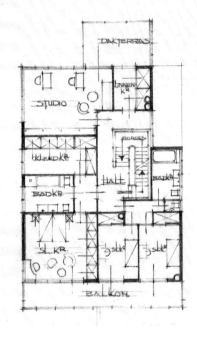

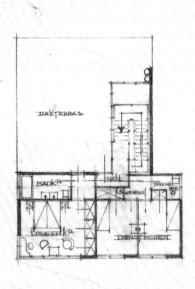

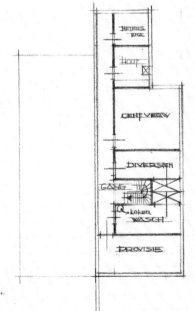

Sonneveld House,
sketch proposal no. 3294-3297,
ca. late December 1930/
early January 1931

Ground floor
First floor
Second floor

Basement

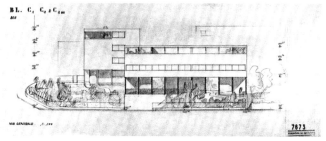

Le Corbusier, design for a detached
and a semi-detached house at the
Weissenhof Siedlung, Stuttgart,
1926-1929
The raised house made manifest

H. van Beek, H.J. Boevé, H. van Gulik, M. de Heer,
P. Merkes, A.H. Sonneveld, and the Atlas Van Stolk.
The heirs of A. van Stolk soon made it clear that they
did not consider it advisable to build new premises for
the Atlas Van Stolk under the deteriorating economic
conditions, and suspended the decision to purchase
land for an indefinite period. De Heer and Van Beek
also turned down the offer soon afterwards. Van Gulik
pulled out not long after, leaving Boevé, who would
have preferred a terrace house on not more than 500 to
600 m² of land, without his two potential neighbours.

The Van Beek House and the setback of
the deepening international economic crisis
One of the candidates, the wealthy Rotterdam merchant
H. van Beek, had also called in Brinkman and Van der
Vlugt. The design process commenced immediately
after the receipt of the sketch of the plot of land on
25 April 1931. It concerned the design of a villa in the
Jongkindstraat with an even larger programme than
what the Sonneveld family wanted, but with similar
compositional and organisational aspects. Six design
variants were examined between 30 April and
18 August, but Van Beek lost his patience with the
Rotterdam city council and his confidence in a rapid
economic recovery. This put an end to the development
of plans for a spectacular villa designed by Brinkman
and Van der Vlugt on a plot of land to the right of The
Sonneveld House. This must have come as a blow to
the architects, because Brinkman and Van der Vlugt
were by now seriously affected by the deepening
international crisis. By the middle of 1931, the only
work they had, apart from a few interiors and renova-
tions and designing the villas in Dijkzigt, was an office
for the Grain Elevator Company. Other sketch plans
were not implemented either. Employees of the time
stated, for instance, that in the second half of 1931,
when they were able to start making plans for the
renovation and expansion of the Diaconessen Hospital
on the Westersingel in Rotterdam (the later Van Dam-
Bethesda Hospital, that was demolished in 1990),

they took the measurements of the old hospital twice
because they were afraid that if they went back to the
office they would be sacked because of the lack of
work.[12] The firm must have cut down drastically at that
time. The remaining knowledge and design capacity
could be largely deployed for the commissions that
were left for the Sonneveld and Boevé Houses.

Third series of sketches
In January 1931 the Sonneveld family discussed the
plan of the house again with Brinkman and Van der
Vlugt. This apparently led them to devise a different
organisation of the house that was necessitated by the
introduction of a double garage inside the building,
which meant raising the living space to the first floor.
At that time cars were usually kept in a detached
garage in the garden. The architect Le Corbusier was
already experimenting with raised homes in the early
1920s, which created space on the ground floor for a
garage, a spacious entrance hall, and personnel: the
home of the Citrohan type (a play on words involving
the Citroën brand of car). Brinkman and Van der
Vlugt had applied the principle of raised housing in
1928 to the Van der Leeuw house on the Kralingse
Plas.

Two sketches for The Sonneveld House were made
in January 1931, but only proposal 3852, sketch A
(22 January 1931) has been preserved. Although it is
a very general sketch, it does contain some interesting
ideas that anticipate the plan of the house that was
eventually built. In its main lines, this organisation
comes close to that of the actual villa, with a clear
demarcation between the living quarters for the family
and the servants' quarters: reception, servants, guest
room and garage on the ground floor; living area,
veranda and kitchen on the first floor; and the family
bedrooms and studio on the second floor. The studio
and the guest room changed places in the final version.
The design of this sketch A reflects a combination of
the two houses that Le Corbusier built at the Weissenhofsiedlung in Stuttgart in 1927.

12 Personal communication, Mr. Goslinga,
Schiedam, 28-10-1992.

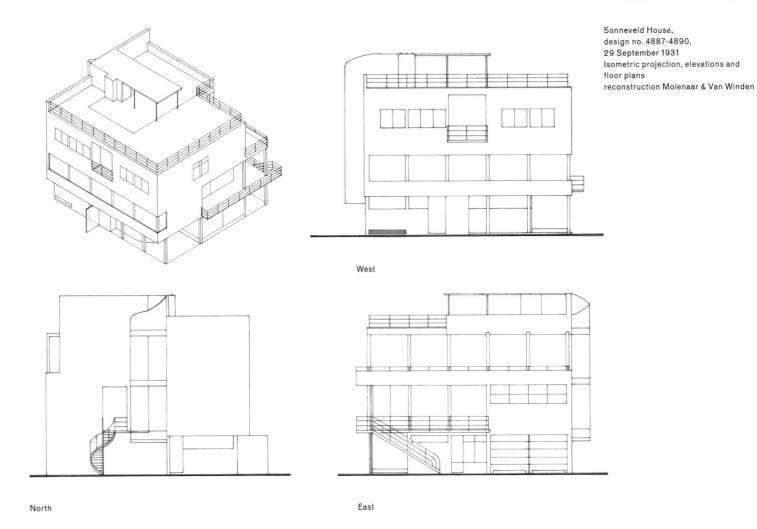

Sonneveld House,
design no. 4887-4890,
29 September 1931
Isometric projection, elevations and
floor plans
reconstruction Molenaar & Van Winden

West

North

East

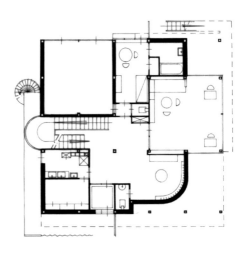

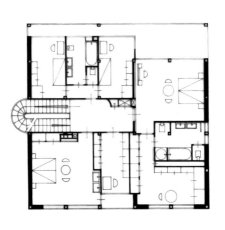

Ground floor
First floor
Second floor

Basement
Roof

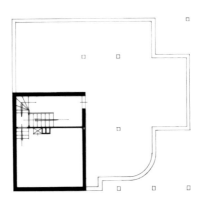
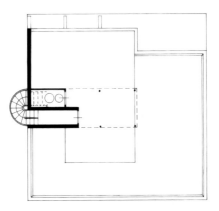

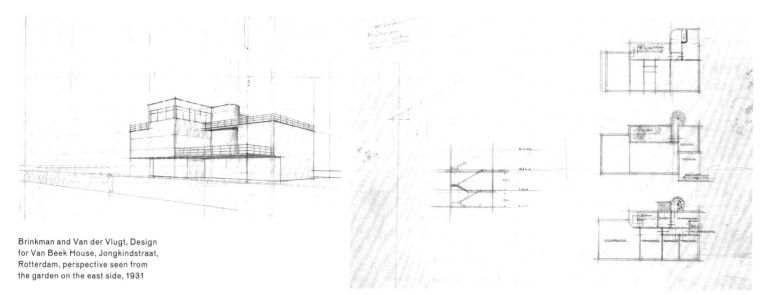

Brinkman and Van der Vlugt, Design
for Van Beek House, Jongkindstraat,
Rotterdam, perspective seen from
the garden on the east side, 1931

Sonneveld House, sketch A
no. 3852, 22 January 1931
Introduction of the raised house

The new arrangement of the programme according to sketch A was elaborated on a larger scale in sketch proposal 4169 of 19 May 1931. The staircase and adjacent servants' and service areas have been moved one metre outwards, and the level with the living area and bedrooms now overhangs the ground floor on either side. The sketch plan is for the second plot of land counting from the Rochussenstraat. The house is to be placed on the northern side of the plot, with the living and dining room on the south where the side garden is located.

Eight days later a completely new plan, no. 4179, was sketched. This plan took the location itself more into account. The plot afforded enough space for the house to be situated more widthways on it. The ground floor entrance is on the street side, while the garage has been moved to the back, with the doors in the side wall. The service and storage rooms are situated in a short corridor, with a transparent studio for the daughters in the southeast corner, adjacent to the garden. From the entrance hall a staircase without a well leads to a central hall on the first and second floor. The living area is divided into a study with an open hearth in the northwest, which can be separated off by a curved partition from the salon in the southwest corner. The latter opens into the dining room, which in turn connects with a veranda in the southeast corner. The kitchen and the servants' rooms are separate on the northeast side, with access via an outdoor staircase. The second floor comprises two large double bedrooms with bathroom, the guest room, and two single children's bedrooms with bathroom. The bedrooms are placed at the corners of this floor, separated by bathrooms or service rooms, to guarantee more privacy. The first and second floor overhang the ground floor to provide enough space for the larger programme of the floors. This will also have been a deliberately con-

trived effect to accentuate parts of the house and to let them float optically in the composition of mass and surfaces, as Gropius and Le Corbusier had also done in the examples mentioned above.

In June 1931 Van der Vlugt visited the Deutsche Bau-Ausstellung in Berlin and the Internationale Hygiene Ausstellung in Dresden to find out about the latest materials, technical installations and interiors with a view to the luxury villa that would soon be under construction. He must also have seen the model house by Mies van der Rohe at the Deutsche Bau-Ausstellung on this occasion – a house in which the living area was designed as an undivided space within which areas were demarcated by free-standing walls and volumes. This was a more radical spatial form than what Van der Vlugt carried out in his designs.

After his return he continued work on the detailed design of the house. During this stage it was mainly the organisation and interior design that was discussed in detail with the family. The fixed and movable furniture is already included on floor plans, as well as the sanitary fittings. The constructional and engineering aspects were studied more closely during this stage, as the steel frame is always indicated precisely in the sketches, and the dimensions of the ducts, piping and wiring are specified.

The four designs that survive from this period down to the end of September are all variations on the main plan outlined above. The staircase was moved to the side wall and the entrance to the garage was moved to the rear wall. This made it possible to spread the living area out across the full width of the front wall on

13   NAI, BROX Archive, dossier work no. 178, documentation Deutsche Bau-Ausstellung, Berlin 1931, dossier work no. 179, documentation Internationale Hygiene Ausstellung, Dresden 1931, both severely damaged by water.

the west side, and across the full depth on the south side. The room looked out on the street side with a wide panoramic view over the new Museumpark to Delfshaven. Since the cars turned behind the house, it was possible to place the villa closer to the northern boundary of the plot so that the living area could benefit to the full from the view of the garden, the sun and the park. The living area increased in size. The bedrooms were divided into children's bedrooms with fittings, a guest room, and a spacious double bedroom with bathroom and dressing room. The servants' rooms were still connected by the main staircase, while an outdoor spiral staircase formed a rather inadequate tradesmen's entrance to the kitchen.

An estimate, including the interior, was made on 4 September 1931. After the calculation of small alternatives, a total budget for the building costs including the interior was drawn up on 11 September. It totalled NLG 105,057, excluding the fee for the architects, the clerk of works and the drawings, expenses and the land.[14]

Sketch design no. 4887-4890 of 29 September is the first to contain sketches of the outside walls. They already contain the characteristic elements of the definitive composition: the balcony strips of the east wall which protrude beyond the main mass, the monumental composition of the front wall, the treatment of the kitchen and garage as a separate part of the building, the static composition of volumes on the northwest side, and the dynamic composition of overlapping terrace and slabs on the southeast side. The return of the pergola on the roof terrace, an element from the very first design sketches, is noteworthy.

The villa was more and more conceived as a rectangular volume with cavities. These cavities provided room for roofed terraces and verandas adjacent to the studio and to a protected entrance area on the ground floor, a veranda adjacent to the dining room on the first floor, and a loggia next to the double bedroom on the second floor. The volume of the building is accentuated as a massive, floating volume on the west side, and an open accumulation of terraces hung inside a frame on the east side. These two principles were intertwined on the south wall, while the north wall is closed, with only the main stairs and the servants' staircase as transparent elements. The characteristic flat wall on the north side also served as a windbreak for the terrace.

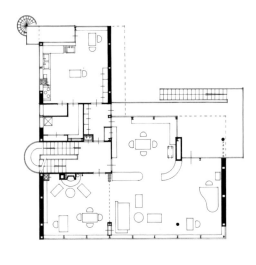

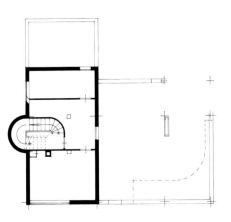

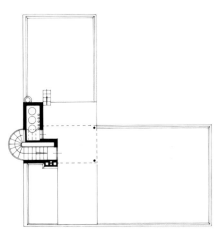

Sonneveld House,
penultimate design no. 4944-4946,
November 1931
Floor plans
reconstruction Molenaar & Van Winden

Ground floor
First floor
Second floor

Basement
Roof

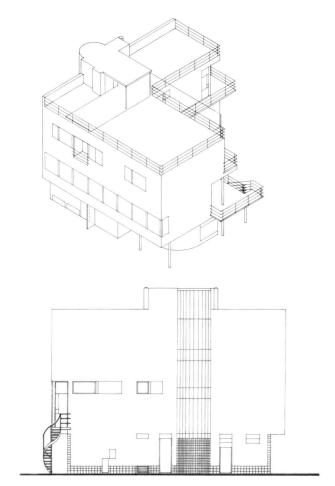

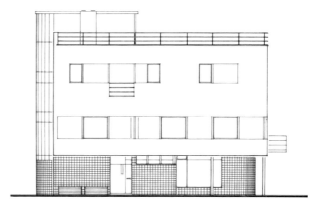

West

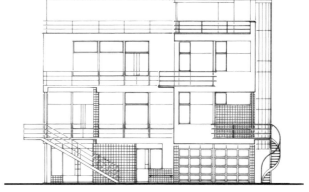

North

East

Sonneveld House,
penultimate design no. 4944-4946,
November 1931
Isometric projection and elevations
reconstruction Molenaar & Van Winden

Penultimate design and purchase of the land

The penultimate design, no. 4944-4946, dates from November 1931. It is the most complex variant of the whole series of designs and looks like a final attempt by Brinkman and Van der Vlugt to satisfy all the requirements and wishes of the family before making definitive decisions. The introduction of an L-shaped building volume made it possible to move the dining room closer to the centre of the floor plan and to situate the veranda in the southeast corner. The kitchen was rotated through ninety degrees to enhance the privacy of the garden. The spiral staircase to the servants' entrance was still clumsily situated, but the kitchen now had a sitting area for the personnel. The studio for the daughters on the ground floor has been given a round outside wall beneath the overhanging living area floor, which made the composition of a floating volume interesting. The floor plans and outside wall designs are very complex and exciting through the direct way in which the consequences of the design choices have been incorporated. This creates the impression that the windows, shutters, doors and window fronts are purely functionally positioned, as in the deckhouse of a liner. This is the most 'maritime'

variant of the designs, appropriate to the search for a modern architectural expression inspired by ship-building, as in the case of Le Corbusier and other contemporaries.

The family now had to wait to be certain that they could purchase the land. Sonneveld had received the offer on 11 August 1931 and on 17 August he immediately addressed a request to the mayor and aldermen of Rotterdam to propose to the city council that the offer of land be sold to him. Eventually the mayor and aldermen were only able to recommend the sale of land to Sonneveld and to Merkes at the end of October. The Rotterdam city council adopted this decision on 26 November 1931 on the terms proposed. Another attempt was made by the community to object to the extremely low price of land by comparison with the prices for other land for building in Dijkzigt and to the fact that there had been no open tender for the plots, but the sale was still approved. Sonneveld and Merkes had to start building within a year, so there was no room for delay.

14 NAI, BROX Archive, work 93 code: fa 3, 1-22.

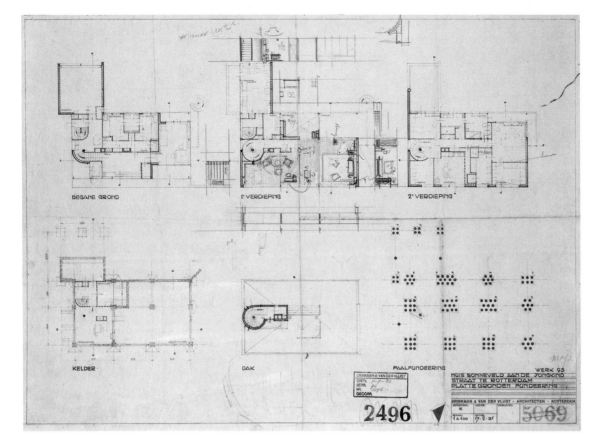

Sonneveld House, tracing of contract
drawing no. 5069, 18 February 1932
Van der Vlugt's interior proposals
for the living area are sketched in red

Intensive discussions took place in December 1931
and January 1932 between Van der Vlugt and the
urban developer Witteveen, who had drawn up the
Dijkzigt Plan, on the consequences of the fact that
several candidates for the plots of land in the Jongkindstraat had withdrawn. The definitive design for The
Sonneveld House was completed immediately afterwards. So after a total of twelve design variants and
further elaborations of the plan, the contract drawings
were finally ready on 18 February 1932. Building permission was granted on 3 June 1932. A month later,
in July 1932, the construction of The Sonneveld House
in the Jongkindstraat commenced.

The definitive design:
refinement and elaboration
The contract drawings of The Sonneveld House
no. 5069 and 5070 of 18 February 1932 incorporate
the experiences from the earlier design studies. A
few radical changes have been introduced that enor-
mously benefitted the functioning of the living area.
The composition of volumes, surfaces and openings is
also more radical, stylised and mannerist. The area for
the hall, stairs and corridors has been kept as compact
as possible by comparison with the earlier designs. By
saving space in this way, the children's bedrooms could
be moved within the main volume, and the protected
terrace with a windbreak was no longer situated at roof

level, but adjacent to one of the children's rooms on
the service wing.

The saving of space that was achieved on the
ground floor made it possible to include two servants'
rooms with their own sanitary fittings, situated in a
separate servants' corridor that was accessible from
the servants' entrance. This ensured maximal separation
of the servants' quarters from the family's home, the
ideal of a classic upper middle-class residence. The
detailed discussions of the interior design and furnishings must have begun at this time. An impression of
the contract drawings has been preserved which
contains Van der Vlugt's ideas about the fixed fittings
and furniture in red pencil. The next stage was to
make detailed drawings on a scale of 1:20 for each
room of the floor plan and projections of the walls.
They were coloured in with a specific colour plan for
each room. All of the bathrooms were also drawn after
the luxurious foreign sanitary fittings had been chosen.
The bathroom for Mr and Mrs Sonneveld included a
shower cabin with a chrome and glass door and several
sprays built into the tiled walls, an unprecedented
luxury by Dutch standards. The sanitary fittings and
tiling in the service rooms were chosen with the same
precision and connected to stop cocks in the chrome
piping from pipe ducts beneath strips of black marble.
Only the colours of the sanitary fittings were somewhat more standard.

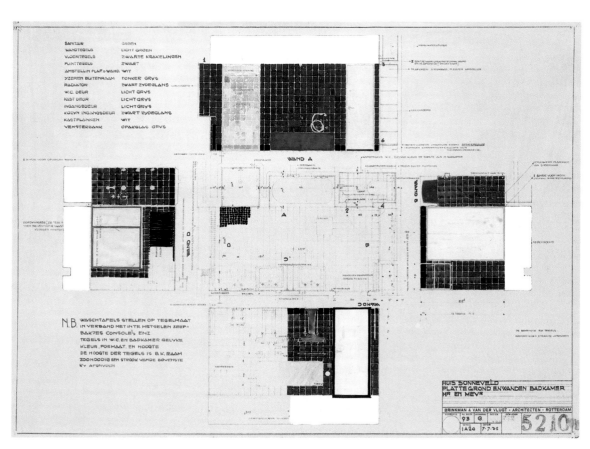

Sonneveld House, tracing of working drawing for the interior of the kitchen, no. 5260, 1 September 1932
Coloured with poster paint

Sonneveld House, tracing of working drawing for the interior of the bathroom of Mr and Mrs Sonneveld, no. 5210, 7 July 1932
Coloured with poster paint

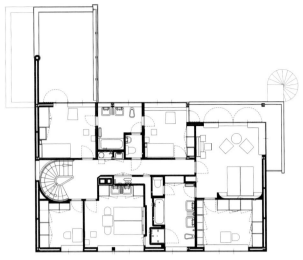

Second floor

Roof

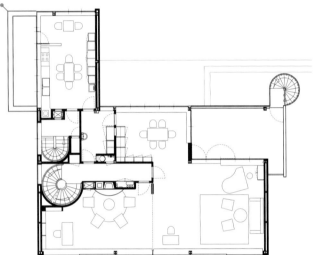

First floor

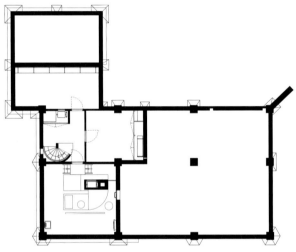

Basement

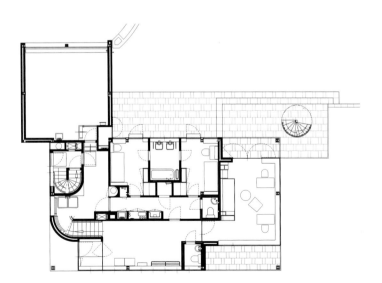

Ground floor

Sonneveld House,
definitive design no. 5069-5070,
18 February 1932
Floor plans, elevations
and cross-sections
reconstruction Molenaar & Van Winden

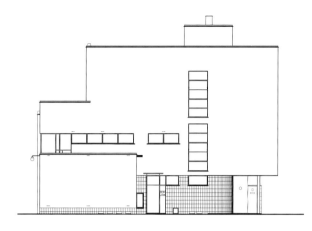

North

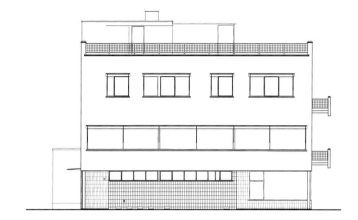

West

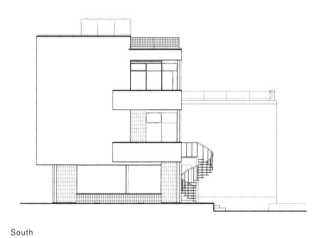

South

East

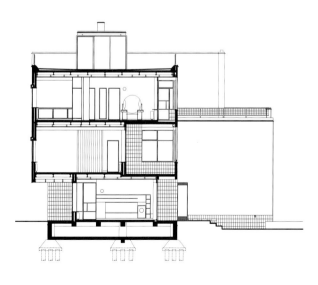

Cross section

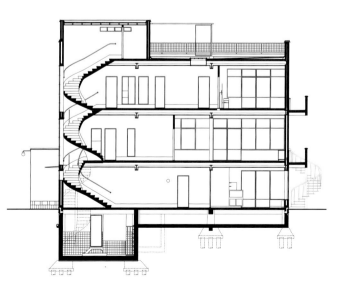

Longitudinal section

59

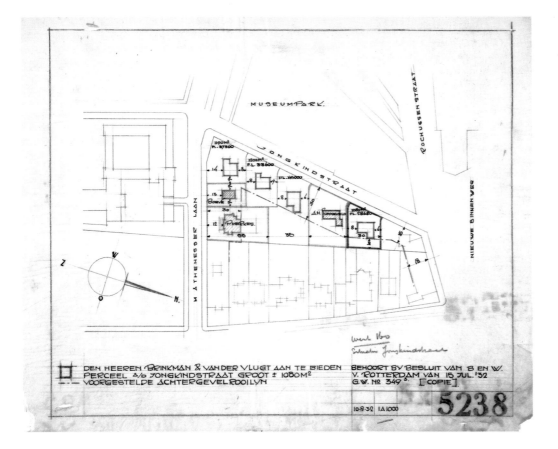

Situation of Dijkzigt Villa Park
with definitive plots of land,
15 July 1932

Sonneveld House under
construction, summer 1932
The fenced-off building site with site
hut.

Sonneveld House under construction,
summer 1932
The builders are working on formwork
and binding the metal reinforcement
for the cellar walls

On 11 May 1932 Brinkman and Van der Vlugt drew
up an estimate, excluding furniture and fittings, on the
basis of the contract drawings 5069 and 5070 and
the contract work 93, for a total of NLG 59,662.36.[15]
The chief clerk A.J. Van der Linden carried out a few
economy cuts in the last week of May, including
awnings and shutters, calculated at a total of NLG
11,500. The final estimate for the villa, excluding
furniture and fittings, stood at NLG 48,112.36.[16]

Another economy measure was proposed on 4 June
to replace the main stairs leading to the roof by a
steel outdoor staircase. Fortunately this was rejected.
The budget for extra items such as glass on balcony
balustrades, tiles against balcony balustrades and
several other items was accepted.[17] On 9 June 1932
the contract price of the firm of F.W. Zonneveld was
fixed at NLG 53,772.40. These budgetary documents
include a comment by Van der Linden: 'The assignment
offered the firm of F.W. Zonneveld for NLG 52,500,
accepted for a sum of NLG 52,600'.[18] Tough bargains
were struck during the crisis. The final sum calculated
by Brinkman and Van der Vlugt on 26 June 1933 [19]
reveals that the total cost for building The Sonneveld
House, including furniture and fittings and fees,
amounted to NLG 114,060[19] (821,661 euros) at modern
rates.

Villa Sonneveld and the inspiration from artistic developments

'For the Netherlands we consider Messrs Brinkman
and Van der Vlugt as pioneers of the views advocated
with little variation by Mallet-Stevens, Le Corbusier
in France – and by Breuer, Gropius and others in
Germany.' This appreciation appeared in a publication
of September 1930 by the Pander furniture firm, which
manufactured fixed panelling and interior furniture
and fittings, about the interior of the Van der Leeuw
House.[20] It applies just as well to The Sonneveld House
as to the Van der Leeuw House. The latter was an
extreme expression of a powerful and wealthy bachelor
who wanted to provide a demonstration of Modernist
housing: the dream of a man with a vocation in the field
of modern architecture, but it was no less radical for a
family like the Sonnevelds to have their home designed
completely in a modern way by Brinkman and Van der
Vlugt. Sonneveld was not originally very interested in
the latest trends in the field of modern art and architecture, whereas the brothers Kees and Dick (M.A.G.) van
der Leeuw (1894-1936) took an active interest in art
and architecture; there are indications that they inspired
their fellow directors to have new homes built and also
informed them about the latest examples in architecture.
Kees van der Leeuw and Leen van der Vlugt were in

15 NAI, BROX Archive, work 93 code:
fa 3, 130-150.
16 NAI, BROX Archive, work 93 code:
fa 3, 151-152.
17 NAI, BROX Archive, work 93 code:
fa 3, 154-155.
18 NAI, BROX Archive, work 93 code:
fa 3, 162-162.

19 J.A. Brinkman and L.C. van der Vlugt
architects, Nieuwe Haven 89. Declaration of fee
and advances no. 970 dated 26 June 1933, work
no. 93, kept in the title deeds of The Sonneveld
House, Volkskracht Rotterdam Foundation Archive.
20 See: *Thuis* 3 (1930) 13.

Sonneveld House under construction,
summer 1932

contact with Walter Gropius from 1925. At the same time that the Van Nelle factory was being built, Gropius was working on the Bauhaus (1925-1926) and the related Meisterhäuser in Dessau.[21] Van der Leeuw and Van der Vlugt had also visited the Exposition des Arts Décoratifs et Industriels Modernes in Paris in 1925,[22] where besides Le Corbusier's striking Pavilion de l'Esprit Nouveau and the avant-garde Russian pavilion by Konstantin Melnikov, they could also see the luxurious Art Déco modernism of a figure like Mallet-Stevens. Kees van der Leeuw reproduced photographs from leading publications and magazines like *Mobilier et Décoration*. This shows that the Van der Leeuw brothers were very interested not only in the principled architecture and furniture of the Bauhaus and Le Corbusier, but also in the comfortable and luxurious applied art of Parisian architects and artists associated with movements like the Union des Artistes Modernes (UAM). Kees and Dick van der Leeuw visited showrooms in Paris and passed their impressions and information on to Van der Vlugt. On 20 December 1928 Dick van der Leeuw wrote to Van der Vlugt to prepare the latter's trip to Paris: 'Don't forget to see Dominique, Désagnat and A.C.A.M. You will find all of these addresses without exception extremely worthwhile'.[23] The catalogues that Van der Vlugt brought back from this trip show the luxurious French Art Déco bourgeois interiors of the day. Van der Vlugt's widow remembered the various trips that she made with her husband to Paris and other places: 'The French, we were always crazy about them. We always went to Paris once a year to look at houses and to talk about improvements,

including the furniture and everyday use'.[24] Van der Vlugt must have become acquainted with Le Corbusier's villas during his trips to Paris and with the architect's idiosyncratic puritan interiors. In January 1932 Kees van der Leeuw and Leen van der Vlugt met Le Corbusier personally when he came to the Netherlands to give lectures in Rotterdam, Delft and Amsterdam. He also visited the Van Nelle factory and flew above the Rotterdam harbour. Le Corbusier remarked on this: 'Mr van der Leo [sic] and his architect Van der Vlugt have built a big factory that is the most beautiful spectacle of the modern era that I know. If the present-day world were to be organised like that, harmony would crown our efforts. ... A delightful proof of the life that is coming, of the beautiful, unconditional purity'.[25]

But he evidently did not stop at Le Corbusier. Van der Leeuw's reproductions also include photographs from books like *Amerika* (1928) and *Rusland-Europa-Amerika* (1929) by the Expressionist architect Erich Mendelsohn, and the publication *Wie Baut Amerika* (1930) by Richard Neutra. He tried to make contact with Neutra in 1930 when he was on a lecture tour in Europe in connection with his book, and invited him to visit Rotterdam.[26] Van der Leeuw hereby came into the possession of photographs of the grandiose house and general practitioner's practice Lovell Health House, that was constructed in the same period as Van der Leeuw's House.

In the light of these contacts, it is not surprising that the designs for the Dijkzigt villas betray the influence of the Meisterhäuser of Gropius, the villas of Le Corbusier in Paris, and Neutra's Lovell Health

House. The design of the comfortable interiors by Brinkman and Van der Vlugt, however, is closer to the heavily stylised examples of French Art Déco interiors from 1925 onwards. All these influences and inspirations are incorporated in The Sonneveld House in a manner that is unique to Brinkman and Van der Vlugt.

An interior full of chrome and colour

The interior of The Sonneveld House can be summed up in three words: hygiene, comfort, and luxury – the well-to-do bourgeoisie's interpretation of the Modern Movement's adage: light, air and space. The design of the house was extremely comfortable because all of the functional requirements of the occupants and the personnel were incorporated in a use of space that was functionally refined down to the tiniest detail. This could also be seen in the details of the fixed furniture and technical fittings, the interiors of the living area, study and bedrooms, and in the spatial organisation of the house with the servant's quarters back to back against the family house.

The atmosphere in the house is most clearly expressed in the colour scheme chosen for each room and the furnishings that were selected to match. The colour scheme of Modern Movement interiors has been simplified over the course of time and tradition to what the most principled of modern architects advocated: a black-white-grey scheme with the addition of accents in primary colours.[27] The fact that the interiors designed by Brinkman and Van der Vlugt contained many natural colours, that no surface is actually really white, and that

21 See: Reginald R. Isaäcs, *Walter Gropius, Der Mensch und sein Werk*, vol. 1, Berlin 1983, 412-413.

22 Van der Vlugt had submitted illustrations of the School of Technology and Industry in Groningen to the Architecture Department and received a bronze medal for them. Kees van der Leeuw attended the exhibition, as can be seen from the photographs he took in the Historical Archive of The Heirs of the Widow J. van Nelle.

23 Letter from M.A.G. van der Leeuw to L.C. van der Vlugt 20 December 1928, work 152, Paris exhibition 1928, NAI, BROX Archive.

24 Notes taken by Jeroen Geurst and Joris Molenaar of an interview with Mrs Jenny Vermaas-Middelburg, the widow of Leen van der Vlugt, Rotterdam, 8-12-1982.

25 See: Le Corbusier, 'Winterreis... Holland', January 1932, translation: Frank de Zwager, in: R. Mens, B. Lootsma, J. Bosman, *Le Corbusier en*

Nederland, Utrecht 1985, 86.

26 See: Thomas S. Hines, *Richard Neutra and the Search for Modern Architecture*, Oxford/New York 1982, 94.

27 It is striking that in his letter to Bakema of 13 August 1964, C.H. Van der Leeuw denies the use of natural tones and beiges by Van der Vlugt, while colour research in his own home in the Kralingse Plaslaan in Rotterdam and especially from the Sonneveld proves the opposite. Van der Leeuw commented on the application of colour for Van Nelle: 'Further cheerful, bright colours for the walls in the offices and factory, a lot of white (with a taboo on off-white). The demand for colour was also a reaction on our part to the black-white-grey scheme that was used at the time by the very principled figures in modern architecture'. See: J.B. Bakema, *L.C. van der Vlugt*, Amsterdam 1968, 14.

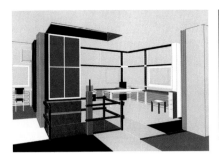

Gerrit Rietveld, Rietveld Schröder
House in Utrecht, 1924
Perspective of the living area with
dining and working table

Le Corbusier, Interior Maison Cook,
Boulogne Bilancourt in Paris, 1926
Isometric projection with colour-
scheme

Buffet in the dining room of the
apartment in the City Flat,
140 Schiedamsevest, Rotterdam,
with the dining room furniture from
the Sonneveld House, 1999

Working drawing no. 5297,
3 October 1932
Interior of girl's bedroom above
the kitchen
Tracing coloured with poster paint

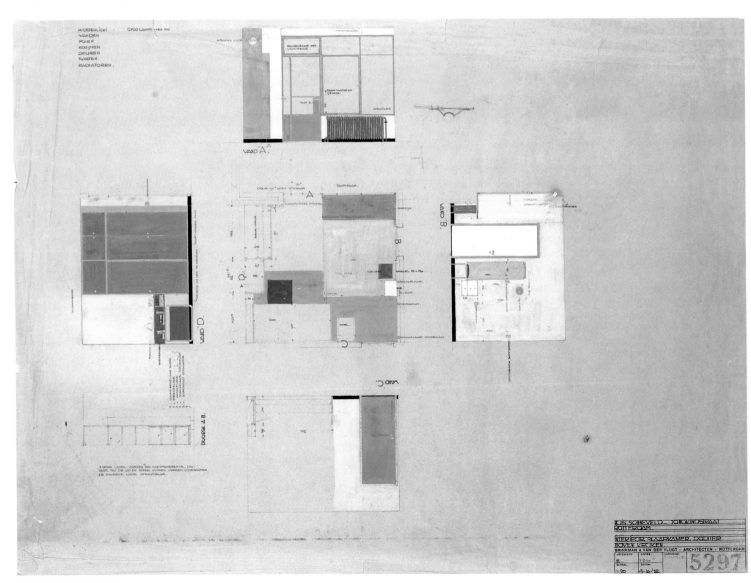

the colours are almost never a primary blue, red and yellow but are softer to harmonise with the upholstery, textures and gloss metal paint in aluminium or bronze in the rooms is something that has to be experienced. Thanks to the research results and the indications of colour on samples of material, it becomes possible to obtain a clearer picture of the colours. This is largely due to the presence of several original books of samples in the archive of Metz & Co. There is no question of an ideologically manifest colour scheme as in the Rietveld-Schröderhuis of 1924, or in the 'contra-constructions' of Van Doesburg from the same period.[28] Nor was there a colour plan that accentuates the space analytically and functionally like that developed in the Bauhaus by Hinnerk Scheper.[29] The determination of mood in the house shows more affinity with the palettes of French Art Déco or the purist artists like Ozenfant and Le Corbusier. Both styles made much use of the monochrome applications of natural and greyish tones, adding colours for accent to strengthen the effect of the whole.[30] Van der Vlugt also applied a much more monochrome palette for each room with a few accents of colour. The colours yellow, silver, grey and brown, bronze and beige predominate in the interior. The use of gloss metal paint in aluminium or bronze in the interior contributes significantly to the atmospheric character of the different rooms. During his training at the Academy of Art and Technical Sciences in Rotterdam, Leen van der Vlugt had become a friend of the decorative painter and draughtsman Jaap Gidding (1887-1955), with whom he worked on earlier commissions for interiors such as the Scala Theatre for Tuschinsky in Rotterdam (1921) and an interior for Dick van der Leeuw in the Westzeedijk in Rotterdam (1926-1927). It is striking to note the similarity between these colours and the palette for which the painter Wim Schumacher (1894-1986) made a name for himself in the 1930s. Dick van der Leeuw was one of this artist's patrons; in 1933 he commissioned him to paint a portrait of his wife, E.J.M. van der Leeuw jonkvrouwe Meyer (1896-1973).[31]

The colourfulness of the interior of The Sonneveld House was described by Jaap Bakema in 1957 in the following words:

Until recently there was still a special atmosphere in each of the bedrooms and the corresponding sanitary space, obtained by colours and details, which at the time were in harmony with the specific condition of a particular member of the family. It was very typical of Van der Vlugt that he spent so much time and attention on reflecting again and again on the living conditions of a family of this kind. The technical fittings of such a house were designed with the same sensitiveness as the choice of the colours for the rooms of the different members of the family. These colours often vary as aluminium paint from silver and grey-green and bronze with red, yellow and blue accents. Van der Vlugt drew on the experiments of De Stijl, Constructivism and Cubism. Never was his work a demonstration or a compromise. He was receptive to the possibilities of his day, including those which until then had only been understood by a few like Rietveld and Oud.[32]

Bakema and Van der Vlugt had never met, but from 1948 on the firm of Brinkman & Van der Vlugt was continued under the name of Van den Broek and Bakema. Bakema had full access to the archives of his predecessors. In 1954 Sonneveld approached the firm of Van den Broek and Bakema to design the interior of a large apartment in the City Flat in the Schiedamse-vest in Rotterdam,[33] where the elderly couple moved in 1955. Bakema must therefore have been in the Jongkindstraat and been able to experience the work of his predecessors in its original state. It can be deduced from this quotation that the interiors were not changed while the Sonneveld family lived there. It is striking how much the interior of the City Flat contained quotations from the interiors of The Sonne-veld House. The Sonnevelds had grown so attached to the atmosphere of the house in the Jongkindstraat that they wanted to take it with them to the Schiedam-sevest!

28 See: Evert van Straaten, *Theo van Does-burg. Schilder en architect*, The Hague 1988.

29 See: Lutz Schöbe, 'Schwarz/Weiß oder Farbe? Zur Raumgestaltung im Bauhausgebäude', in: *Das Bauhausgebäude in Dessau 1926-1999*, Basel 1998.

30 This parallel has already been mentioned in connection with the use of colour in the De Bruyn House in Schiedam in: Elly Adriaansz, Joris Molenaar, 'Witte villa blijkt kleurrijk. Reconstructie polychroom interieur villa Van der Vlugt', in: *Architectuur Bouwen* 6 (1990) 1, 11-16. All the same, the discoveries in The Sonneveld House indicate that this parallel should not be extended too literally.

31 See: Jan van Geest, *Wim Schumacher. De meester van het Grijs*, Arnhem 1991.

32 See: J.B. Bakema, *L.C. van der Vlugt*, Amsterdam 1968, 11-12.

33 This was a double apartment on the top floor of the City Flat, 140 Schiedamsevest in Rotterdam, designed by the architect Pouderoyen. The apartment was later divided into two again and was recently renovated. Most of the original interior was destroyed at that time.

Yew hedge along Jongkindstraat
shortly after it was planted, 1933

The western section of the garden
in 1933

The Garden of The Sonneveld House

Part of an unusual ensemble

Eric Blok and Birgit Lang

Immediately after the completion of The Sonneveld House in 1933, a garden was laid out around the villa as an integral part of the *Gesamtkunstwerk*. The garden and the house formed a carefully composed entity, and the garden, like the house and its interior, was an unusual design in terms of quality and style.

Historical data

The original garden layout for The Sonneveld House is well documented. Three plan drawings of the garden by Brinkman and Van der Vlugt are still in existence. The first covers the whole plot of around 1,700 m^2 and indicates the position and construction of the paths, steps, retaining walls and stepping stones. The plant areas and hedges are also included by way of indication. The two accompanying detailed drawings refer to the paths and the garden fence.[1]

More than twenty black and white photographs – dating mainly from 1933 – cover almost the whole of the original garden. They not only show that the architectural elements were carried out in accordance with the plans, but they also give an impression of what the character and the spatial organisation of the garden were really like. The photographs also provide valuable information about the use and combination of plants, their size, shape and flowers. Some plants can even be clearly identified. Archival documents indicate that the young garden architect Murk Leverland (1904-1964) was involved in designing the garden,[2] though it is impossible to determine exactly what he contributed to the final result because his design drawings have not been found and little is known about his person or his oeuvre.[3]

Original garden layout

The basis for the unity of The Sonneveld House and its garden lay in the well-considered positioning of the villa on the lot: the house was built close to the northern boundary, which enabled the whole garden to bathe in sunlight. The vertical elements in the garden on the other three sides were at a distance from the building, so that the garden gave the house functional and compositional space: on the one hand, it guaranteed optimal daylight indoors, on the other hand the house was dominant in the garden as a cubic object.

A lot of attention was devoted to a fluid transition from indoors to outdoors. Recesses in the outer wall and the large glass wall in the southern elevation bring about an interpenetration of indoors and outdoors. Most of the rooms have direct access to the garden or to one of the balconies or roof terraces. The garden acquired the character of a large outside room through the straight, closed walls (the yew hedges) and the walls of the house, most of which rose straight up from the flat surface of the lawn without any transition. The rectangular recesses of the building were repeated in the garden by recesses in the hedges and in the terraces with retaining wall. This device contributed to a large extent to the integration of the house and the garden.

The retaining wall between the terraces and the southern boundary of the land created a caesura not only by bringing out the gradient in the garden. To the west of this wall the garden was rather static. The lines were here straight and sharp, usually without any transitional zone between vertical and horizontal elements. This part of the garden was dominated by lawn and evergreen yew hedges, whose shape and size were established and maintained by pruning and mowing. The part of the garden east of the retaining wall had dynamic lines with gentle curves. There was a gradual transition from low shrubs to taller plants, and the borders of the lawn were softened by a profusion of plants growing over them. The plants were allowed to grow freely here, and the types chosen had a pronounced annual cycle of growth, flowering, going to seed and dying or shedding their leaves.

The division of the garden into a dynamic, natural eastern half and a static, architectural western half was not taken to extremes. A static element was contributed to the eastern part by the paving of the terraces, a number of evergreen bushes and the lawn, while

1 Drawings nos. 5341,5342, 5314, work no. 93 (Sonneveld House), Brinkman & Van der Vlugt Archive, Netherlands Architecture Institute.

2 The list of drawings for work no. 93, Brinkman & Van der Vlugt Archive, mentions two plans by Murk Leverland, both on a scale of 1:100 (nos 2380 and 2411). These drawings have unfortunately not been traced.

3 For biographical information on Murk Leverland: A. Schippers, 'Genealogie Leverland', in: *Mensen van vroeger. Onafhankelijk maandblad voor de beoefening van de genealogie*, 6/7 (1978/1979) no. 2 (April/May), 6 and 43-44. Interviews with relatives and acquaintances of Leverland have not produced any further information about his work as a garden architect.

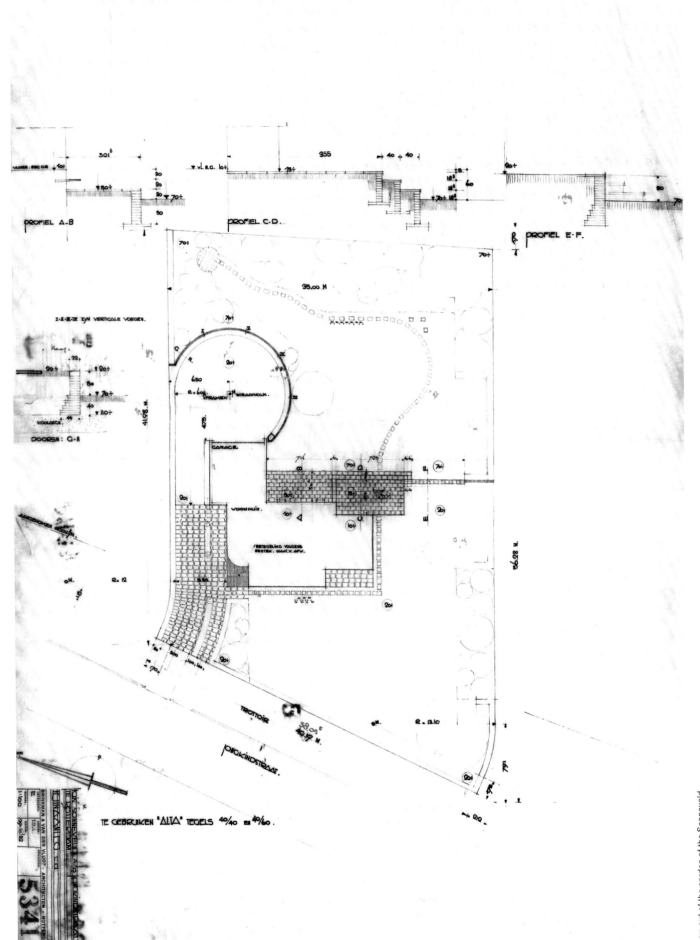

Lay-out of the garden of the Sonneveld
House, drawing by Brinkman and
Van der Vlugt, 1932

Perennial borders in the eastern part of the garden, 1933

dynamic elements were incorporated in the western half, such as a (deciduous) birch.

The entrance and the garage drive were strictly demarcated from the other parts of the garden, which were exclusively for private use by the occupants and their guests. The drive in the original plan followed the curve of the northern boundary and then skirted the house to the turning circle in front of the garage. There were two separate gates for pedestrians and cars. The drive was marked off from the parallel pedestrian path by a narrow decorative border. This decorative border was only interrupted opposite the front door and the tradesmen's entrance. The whole entrance was extremely sober in design and was dominated by architectural elements: the house itself, the paving, the yew hedges and the upright yews.

Importance for garden history
The garden is exceptionally interesting from the perspective of garden history, and not only because of the excellent documentation. In the Netherlands and elsewhere in Europe, the decade of the 1930s was a lively era in the development of modern design principles in accordance with the social, functionalist and aesthetic ideas that had arisen in the Modern Movement.[4] The Sonneveld garden can be regarded as an early example of a Dutch garden that endeavoured to give shape to the functionalist ideas for outdoor space and at the same time to find an appropriate response to the architecture of a house built in the Modernist style.[5] Typical structural characteristics of a modern, functionalist garden layout that can be found in the garden of The Sonneveld House are:[6]

the orientation of the garden towards the use of the house and its demand for daylight;
• the attempt to achieve a smooth transition from indoors to outdoors;
• the correspondences to the lines of the house;
• the essentially sober and simple layout;
• the subordination of the vegetation to architectural aims;
• the limited assortment of plants, especially in the western half of the garden;
• the application of modern building materials, such as metal gauze for the garden fence, sand-lime brick for the retaining walls, and concrete tiles for the turning circle in front of the garage.

4   Compare, for example: C. Tannard, *Gardens in the modern landscape,* Westminster 1938; D. Imbert, *The modernist garden in France,* New Haven (Conn.) 1993; O Valentien, *Zeitgemässe Wohngärten,* Munich 1932.

5   Many other Dutch garden and landscape architects only started to work in a modern functionalist style at a later date. The collaboration between the garden architect Mien Ruys and architects connected with the Modern Movement only began in 1940 (B. Zijlstra, *Mien Ruys. Een leven als tuinarchitecte,* Nederlandse Tuinenstichting/Stichting 'Tuinen Mien Ruys' 1990.) The garden architect J.T.P. Bijhouwer became a member of the 'Opbouw' group in the 1930s and of 'De 8' in the 1940s, but his garden designs from that period only correspond to a very limited extent to the principles of modern design (M. Witsenburg, *Prof.dr.ir.J.T.P. Bijhouwer als tuinarchitect,* Wageningen 1983.) G. Bleeker's work only displays functionalist features after the Second World War, although a move in that direction could be detected earlier on (E. Blok, *Nederlandse tuinarchitectuur III. Jongere Tuinkunst 1900-1940,* Nederlandse Tuinenstichting 1992.) In 1933 a garden design by the Belgian landscape architect Jean Canneel-Claes attracted a good deal of attention. It was regarded as a successful example of the stylistic and functional integration of a modern home with its garden (K. Limperg, 'Een tuin van de belgise tuinarchitekt Jean Canneel-Claes', in: *De 8 en Opbouw,* 4 (1933), no. 6, 43-46.)

6   Compare: C.S. Oldenburger-Ebbers, A.M. Backer, E. Blok, *Gids voor de Nederlandse tuin- en landschapsarchitectuur. Deel West.* Rotterdam 1998, 58-59.

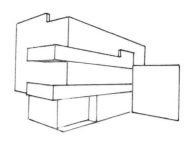

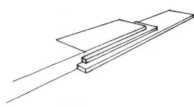

Puck on the retaining wall between front and back garden, 1933

Staggering in facade, fences and terrace, drawing: SB4, 2000

The mixed borders in the eastern half of the garden are clearly inspired by the older tradition of the Arts and Crafts Movement. Borders of this kind, as they were used in the Netherlands especially from the 1920s, betrayed a great attention to the picturesque composition of plants and were intended to achieve well-defined colour effects.[7]

The situation in 2000 and the restoration of the garden

The main lines of the original garden layout were still found on the site in September 2000. The retaining walls and terraces were still there – albeit damaged by subsidence – as well as a piece of the original yew hedge along the Jongkindstraat and a few original shrubs and trees. The garden was in a neglected state through lack of maintenance, and the clarity of the layout was considerably blurred by the spontaneous wild shoots of trees. Moreover, the construction of Rochussenstraat had modified the northern boundary of the plot and definitively changed the entrance.

In the meantime specific interventions (removal of wildshoots, pruning, raising of the subsidence,

replanting of the hedges, fresh laying of the lawn) have restored the original visual and spatial situation as far as possible. Terraces, retaining walls and the garden fence could be reconstructed on the basis of the surviving drawings and of the remains that were found.

An attempt has been made to bring back the original details within this basic framework. This entails the selection of a historically justified range of plants and their authentic grouping. The historical photographs were used as the point of reference. However, it was not possible to determine the original varieties or cultivated variants (cultivars) on the basis of the photographs. In order to reconstruct the original assortment as accurately as possible, the standard literature of the time was consulted and nursery catalogues of plant varieties and cultivars were traced that were available in the Netherlands in 1932 and were probably familiar to and used by Murk Leverland.

The restoration of the main lines of the garden layout and of the details makes this unique ensemble of house, garden and interior complete for the second time.

7 Compare the work of the English garden architect Gertrude Jekyll, which was very well known in the Netherlands.

Creepers against the garage wall,
1935

The garden on south side of house in 1933. In the foreground: linear rose bed. In the background: informal planting along the east boundary

The Sonneveld House

Photography by Jannes Linders
Spring 2001

Garden in October 2000, view of the
north-east corner of the lot

Sonneveld House seen from the corner
of Rochussenstraat and Jongkindstraat

Jongkindstraat with view of the north
and west elevations

Rear view of the house

North elevation with left the trade entrance and right the main entrance

North elevation with the etched, 'frosted glass' staircase window

Part of the east elevation with the double garage

South and east elevations with stairs to
garden room on first floor

Reconstruction of the entrance hall
with original furnishings

Reconstruction of the studio, with the
newly upholstered sofa in blue cotton
repp by Allan & Co and the cupboard
with built-in tap

Reconstruction of the kitchen
with the kitchen unit designed by
Piet Zwart

Telephones

The telephones are one of the few products which immediately date the interior of The Sonneveld House to long before the Second World War. Soon after the family went to live there, the house contained no fewer than twelve telephones: two for the external line – one in the parents' bedroom and one on Mr Sonneveld's desk in his studio – and ten intercom telephones – in the hall, the studio, the servants' quarters, the study, the dining room, the kitchen, the parents' bedroom, and the daughters' bedrooms. Since the external and internal lines were completely independent of one another, there were two telephones side by side in the study and in the bedroom of Mr and Mrs Sonneveld.

The telephone network in Rotterdam, like that in Amsterdam and The Hague, was still run by the local authority in the 1930s, while all the other networks in the Netherlands had already been taken over by the State. The Rotterdam exchange had been automated by this time, as can be seen from the dial, but this only applied to calls within the city; all other connections had to be made through the telephone exchange.[1]
There were 22,615 subscribers in Rotterdam at the beginning of 1934, which meant that 1 in 25 of the residents of Rotterdam had a telephone – more than a thousand less than in 1933. The crisis had forced many households to cancel what must have been a recent connection. A connection cost NLG 96 a year in 1931, an exceptionally large sum of money at the time, which excluded the price of long distance and international calls.
The choice of the type of telephone for the public telephone network was extremely limited for subscribers. The local authority had a contract with Ericsson, which meant that all equipment had to be purchased from this Swedish company, although the telephones were actually manufactured in the Netherlands (in Rijen, North Brabant). The black telephone had a rather old-fashioned look about it, certainly by comparison with the intercom telephones, and had two gold-coloured horizontal stripes on the base.

This was characteristic of Ericsson telephones. Typical for Rotterdam was the second receiver to enable a third party to listen in to the conversation.
The more modern-looking intercom system in The Sonneveld House consisted of black wall models – the very latest thing in 1933 – and black and white table models. Incidentally, intercoms were not a recent invention, but they were usually bought by businesses; it was a luxury item for private use. The internal telephones were manufactured by Siemens & Halske, the firm with by far the most varied range at the time. They were manufactured in the Netherlands from 1932 onwards after Siemens had concluded a contract with the Heemaf factory in Hengelo.

JC+MST

1   Automation of the Rotterdam telephone network was completed im 1932; the State assumed control of the exchange in 1940. See also: J.H. Schuilenga, J.D. Tours, J.G. Visser, J. Bruggeman (eds), *Honderd jaar telefoon. Geschiedenis van de openbare telefonie in Nederland 1881-1981*, The Hague 1981 and *Geschiedenis van de telefoondienst in de stad Rotterdam* [Rotterdam 1981].

Reconstruction of the kitchen with clock and telephone. The goods lift is visible on the right

Reconstruction of the kitchen with the kitchen unit manufactured by Bruynzeel to a design by Piet Zwart. Probably introduced in the 1930s to replace the Mauser kitchen cupboards

Kitchen curtains

The curtains that hung in front of the window of the large kitchen on the first floor of The Sonneveld House were decorated with a simple print pattern consisting of red and grey squares and rectangles. The same pattern, but in yellow and grey, could be found in the service room and the linen room. The simple motif on these curtains recalls the pattern that is etched in the staircase window.

The curtains were supplied by the firm of Metz & Co, which also provided most of the other fabrics in the villa.[1] The material appears in a brochure of this progressive and luxurious interior decoration store. It was designed by Elise Djo Bourgeois, and was priced at NLG 5.50 in 1930 in the series 'Sunfirm Cretonnes and Linens'. It was presented that same year at the 'Third International Exhibition of Contemporary Industrial Art', an exhibition of mainly modern metalwork and textiles which could be seen at four different venues in the United States.[2] The geometric pattern gives the fabric a modern, severe look, but the bright colours and loosely woven linen material also make it cheerful and natural. Close inspection shows that the material has been hand-printed; it is not very difficult to trace slight irregularities. The production of this exclusive material was apparently not large enough to justify the expensive investment involved in fully mechanical printing, but it is likely that it was the very craft-conscious character of printing by hand which was appreciated.

In 1933 this fabric was not the very latest of what was available in this field. Metz & Co had been experimenting with similar modern printed cretonnes for more than ten years.

The first artist with whom Joseph de Leeuw, the director of Metz, had been cooperating since 1922 was the Hungarian De Stijl artist Vilmos Huszár, who designed six patterns consisting of blocks and stripes. These designs were still on sale at Metz in the 1930s. Joseph de Leeuw had a special relation with the French artist Sonia Delaunay; after selling her French-produced fabrics in Amsterdam for several years, his company started producing her designs itself around 1930. At this period Metz & Co also maintained contacts with a few other French designers, including Elise Djo Bourgeois and Jean Burkhalter.

Metz was not the only firm to produce modern interior textiles in the Netherlands.[3] The firm of Van Vlissingen in Helmond already had several collections of modern print curtains in 1927 and 1928. And the Dutch designers Cornelis van der Sluys, Thom Posthuma and Adriaan van der Plas designed simple geometric patterns to match a collection of wallpaper that was marketed by Rath & Doodeheefver (Schiebroek). Weaving mill De Ploeg in Bergeyk was also producing fabrics in the late 1920s which were very popular among the Modern Movement architects for their bright colours and simple patterns.

JC+MST

1   P. Timmer, *Metz & Co. De creatieve jaren*, Rotterdam 1995.

2   Exh. Cat. *Decorative Metalwork and Cotton Textiles. Third International Exhibition of Contemporary Industrial Art*, Boston (The Museum of Fine Arts) 1930.

3   M. Simon Thomas, 'Cretonnes. De Vormgeving van bedrukt katoen voor het interieur in Nederland 1875-1940', *Katoendruk in Nederland*, [Tilburg/Helmond] 1989, 85-110 (exh.cat. Tilburg (Nederlands Textielmuseum Tilburg), Helmond (Gemeentemuseum Helmond).

Staircase, flight leading from entrance hall
to first floor

The laundry troughs and high-gloss chrome drying racks under the stairs to the first floor

Reconstruction of the library with many of
the original books belonging to the Sonneveld
family, Gispen desk no. 601, the original
Gispen office chair no. 355 and the original
Gispen tables no. 506-508

Overhead lighting with a row of Philinea
lamps in the library, and replica of hanging
lamp no. 63 designed by W.H. Gispen

Reconstruction of the living room looking towards the dining room and the library with replicas of the fireside chairs upholstered with peach cloth in Bart van der Leck red

Reconstruction of the living room with replicas of the chairs upholstered with sand-coloured, striped épinglé, brown chenille curtains, and a replica of the original SAFT carpet designed by Elise Djo Bourgeois

The leatherette harmonica wall and an
off-white chenille curtain act as flexible walls
on the living level

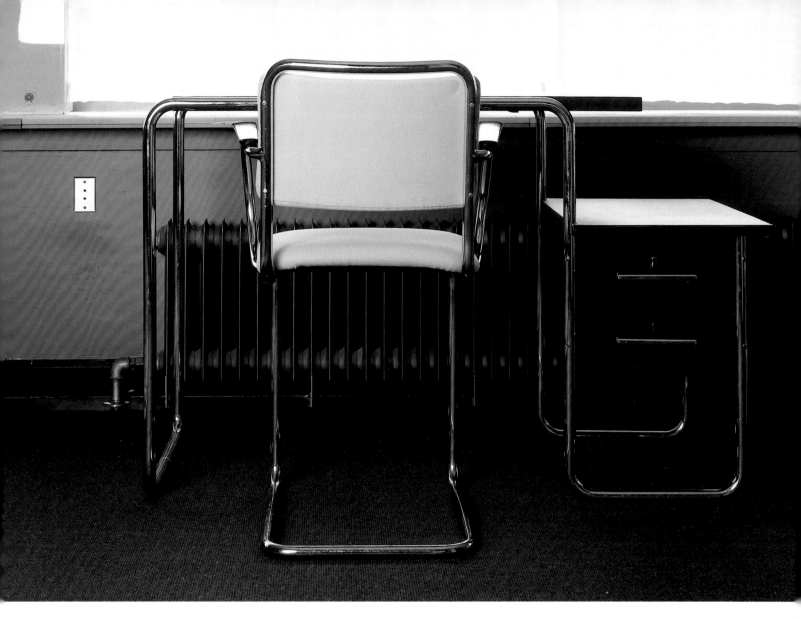

Mrs Sonneveld's desk, model B91
by architect Béwé, produced by the
Thonet company and the original
office chair upholstered with perch
cloth in Bart van der Leck yellow

Reconstruction of the dining room with
the woven carpet in Bart van der Leck yellow
and velvet curtains in Bart van der Leck blue,
and a replica of the Gispen tea trolley no. 555
in Bart van der Leck red

Wall clock

A good example of the many hypermodern technical gadgets with which The Sonneveld House was already fitted during its construction is provided by the electrical wall clocks that could be found all over the house in conspicuous places. The clocks were plastered into the walls and directly connected to the mains. Just how unusual this was can be seen from the fact that – with the exception of the house designed for Van der Leeuw, one of the directors of the Van Nelle factory, by Brinkman and Van der Vlugt – no other case of a private house is known with an installation of this kind, nor is it mentioned in any publication on modern interiors from the period.

The clock face was probably designed by Brinkman and Van der Vlugt. It is a very simple design, which made it easy to read even at a distance. The numerals have been replaced by simple lines, and the hands are in fact no more than straight lines. The clock is not decorated in any way. There is an undated and unsigned design sketch for a clock face in the Brinkman and Van der Vlugt archive that is virtually identical to that of the clocks in The Sonneveld House. Only the hands are much less geometric on the sketch: they taper at the end and have rounded corners.

The clock mechanism came from the German AEG factory and was enclosed in a sort of tin that was set into the wall. This box was fitted with a lid so that the mechanism was still accessible if the clock had to be adjusted. Unfortunately over the years all the clocks and clock faces have disappeared. Only one of the tins has been found.

The clock faces were made of glass by the firm of A.C. Degens, the company that also supplied the etched glass for the staircase window in The Sonneveld House.[1] It is difficult to see in the old photographs, but the lines to indicate the hours were probably painted on the back of the glass clock face. A smooth background was then introduced behind it, perhaps in the same colour as the wall where the clock was hung. This hid the mounting of the clock on the wall beautifully: the front was unpainted and easy to keep clean.

Although the network of clocks was certainly unique, the illustrated literature of the early 1930s contains more examples of functionalist clocks with a similarly austere design.[2] However, they also contain many illustrations of more exuberant models inspired by the Amsterdam School style and clocks in shapes based on the traditional historical styles. The modern models often have a clock face made of glass in which the hours have been etched, but metal was regularly used too. The shape of these contemporary electrical clocks was geometric: circular, rectangular or square. As in the case of the clocks in The Sonneveld House, the numerals were often replaced by lines, and there was no decoration of any kind.

JC+MST

1   This is shown by the final bill presented by Brinkman and Van der Vlugt to Sonneveld on 26 June 1933 (Brinkman and Van der Vlugt archive).
2   See, for example: W.R., 'Wandklokken', *Het Landhuis* 28 (1933), 864 or E.M.R., 'Nieuwe Kunst', *De vrouw en haar huis* 29 (1934-1935), 250; and the catalogues of Metz & Co and De Bijenkorf from this period in the Amsterdam Municipal Archive.

Dinner service

Leonard Kooij at the table with his grandmother, Mrs Sonneveld, ca. 1954

When there was no company, the Sonneveld family used a simple dinner service, of which a few dinner and soup plates have been preserved. The plates are made of a cream-coloured porcelain with an almost minimal two-line decoration around the edge: a thin black line, and a slightly wider silver-coloured one. Apart from the material and the silver line, which gives the service a somewhat more elegant appearance, it is a simple, no-nonsense design.

The service was made by Pirkenhammer, a ceramics factory in Bohemia (now part of the Czech Republic). Porcelain vases and dinner services were manufactured there from 1807, but the firm is no longer in existence today. Besides the factory seal, some of the plates have a second seal, that of Junger-hans, the shop in Rotterdam where the service was purchased. It is very likely that it was already available from Jungerhans before 1933. It is therefore not certain whether the service was purchased by the Sonneveld family when they moved to the new villa, or whether they already used it in their old house.

The range available at Jungerhans in 1933 included not only the many models decorated with floral and other decorative motifs, but also services that were even more simple and modern than the dinner service that the Sonneveld family chose; for example, the products made by De Sphinx in Maastricht or Ram in Arnhem. Apparently Mrs Sonneveld preferred something a little more distinguished to these sober models that looked like kitchenware.

Jungerhans was one of the most important and best-known specialist shops in Rotterdam. There were no other shops with a comparable range, and the only competitors to a certain extent were De Bijenkorf and Vroom & Dreesmann.[1] The Jungerhans clientèle, the well-to-do class, came from all over the country in the 1930s. The people who emigrated to the Dutch East Indies formed a special group of customers. Jungerhans had a special section for them, and could boast years of experience in shipping furniture and other household items to the former Dutch colonies in the East.

The firm of Jungerhans was founded in 1882 by Anton (H.R.A.) Jungerhans. It sold luxury and domestic articles, furniture, light fittings, household linen, and just before the Second World War broke out it added cast-iron fireplaces to the range. The collection also included 'modern' products of applied art, but by far the largest part of the collection came from well-known, large factories.

Right from the start, however, the most important items to be sold at Jungerhans were ceramics and glass. In the 1930s it stocked ceramics and porcelain from De Sphinx, Mosa and De Porceleyne Fles, as well as glass from the glass factory in Leerdam and the Kristalunie in Maastricht. Besides Dutch products, it also sold a lot of imports from the German-speaking countries — such as tableware from Rosenthal and Pirkenhammer — as well as many items from France, England and Italy. In a few cases the models were decorated exclusively for Jungerhans, and in that case the name of the shop appeared on the tableware. Very occasionally there was not enough room to include the name of the manufacturer.

JC+MST

1   The information about the Jungerhans firm is based on a conversation with the firm's former owners, Mr and Mrs W.B.M. Jungerhans, on 28 February 2000; press release distributed on the occassion of the opening of A. Jungerhans Corner Coolsingel/Binnenweg Rotterdam from June 1953; *Jungerhans 1882-1982. 100 jaar Jungerhans in pocket formaat* from May 1982.

Reconstruction of the master bedroom with
Gispen table and chairs no. 407

Reconstruction of the dining room with the original dining room suite adapted by Gispen to the Sonnevelds' specifications. The table incorporates a bell for summoning servants. In the background the display case containing art glass from the Leerdam glassworks

Vases

Dining room display case with
B (smooth) glassware by K.P.C. de Bazel,
vases by A.D. Copier, water jug by
C. de Lorm, and small vase by
H.P. Berlage, 2001

The photographs that were taken soon after the completion of The Sonneveld House show that the interior was brightened up with a number of flower-filled vases. They were probably all from the Leerdam glass factory and designed by Andries Copier.[1]
An exemplar of Copier's well-known spherical vase, filled with chrysanthemums, can be seen on the round table in the sitting room. It is a variation of the design from around 1930, with an etched lip. The large oval vase with lilies standing on Mrs Sonneveld's desk in the library can be clearly identified as a Copier design. It was produced in series from 1928 and was available in different sizes: the exemplar in the Sonneveld, standing about 18 cm tall, was one of the largest versions. A cubic vase in matt glass apparently stood on the salon table in the sitting room. This type of vase was difficult to produce and was only in production for a short while around 1930.

Copier was the only designer to be permanently employed in the Leerdam glass factory. He went to work for the firm in 1914 at the age of thirteen, and in the course of time developed to become an all-round designer of both hand-made unica as well as vases and tableware produced in series. Copier also did almost all the graphic work for the firm, such as advertising folders and brochures. His first designs, including the comfrey tableware and various vases and bowls, were taken into production in 1923. Although Copier's models were relatively simple almost from the start, this is particularly true of the vases that he designed around 1928-1930. The best-known are the spherical vases, whose basic shape is a pure sphere, slightly flattened in order to be able to stand and provided with a small opening at the top. They were manufactured in different sizes and finishes.

The director of the glass factory, P. M. Cochius, had implemented an emphatically artistic and social policy ever since 1912. He was one of the first Dutch entrepreneurs to work intensively with artists. His aim was to produce affordable, well-designed products that were available for everyone. In 1924 he was one of the initiators and the first chairman of the Union for Art in Industry (BKI), a collaborative enterprise involving manufacturers, distributors and artists. The directors of the firm of Metz & Co and of N.V. Gispen's Fabriek voor Metaalbewerking were also among the first and most active members of the BKI. Leerdam glass was propagated in the 1920s and 1930s in all the progressive interior magazines and books, where the factory regularly placed attractively designed advertisements. The products themselves could be obtained in a number of places. The Sonneveld family may have bought their glass vases from Metz & Co, where they ordered so many other interior items, but it is more likely that they simply bought the vases from the Jungerhans company. Leerdam glass was also obtainable from the many arts and crafts businesses that flourished in Rotterdam around 1930.

JC+MST

1   R. Liefkes, *Copier – Glasontwerper/ Glaskunstenaar*, The Hague [1989]. A. van der Kley-Blextoon, *Leerdam glas 1878-1930*, Lochem-Ghent 1999.

Staircase window

A striking detail in the interior of The Sonneveld House is the etched matt glass window on the landing. Each of the ten panes of glass that combine to form this elongated staircase window is decorated with the same simple geometric pattern made up of squares and rectangles. A similar type of staircase window can be seen in the house on the corner of the Mathenesserlaan and the Jongkindstraat where the Chabot Museum is now housed.

The panes of glass were supplied by the Degens company in Rotterdam.[1] Brinkman and Van der Vlugt, and probably Mr Sonneveld himself as well, were well acquainted with this firm because a few years earlier it had supplied the unusual blue glass for the furniture in the directors' rooms in the Van Nelle factory. The 'N.V. Maatschappij Ned. Stoom-, Glas- en Spiegelfabriek v.h. A.C. Degens' was founded in 1902. Its predecessor was the glass insurance company Securitas that Degens had established four years earlier. In fact the firm was not a glass factory at all, but it imported large sheets of glass — sometimes as large as 3 x 6 metres — from factories in Belgium. The Rotterdam company then cut the glass to size, sold it, and decorated it for commemorative or advertising purposes if required. This decoration could be done in a variety of ways. Besides stained glass, it was also possible to have the glass silver-plated, painted, sandblasted or etched. If it was to be sandblasted, parts of the glass were covered with filter paper (soaked in adhesive) before being sprayed with a hard sandy blast; if it was to be etched, the covering material was varnish and the glass was dipped in an acid bath. In both cases the uncovered parts of the glass were affected and roughened. The longer the sheet of glass was sandblasted or kept in acid, the deeper the layer that was removed. The advantage of etching above sandblasting was that it allowed for many more nuances. That is why the glass for The Sonneveld House was etched.

It is not clear who designed the pattern of the window in The Sonneveld House. It may have been designed by the Brinkman and Van der Vlugt firm of architects, but no sketches have been found in the archive to corroborate this hypothesis. The Degens company did not have any designers of its own; there was a draughtsman, but all he did was to transfer the design to the glass.

JC+MST

1   The information about A.C. Degens comes from an interview with Mr J.C.A. de Kok, former proprietor of A.C. Degens and Securitas, on 30 March 2000 in Capelle aan den IJssel, and from a letter dated 16 June 1909 from A.C. Degens to Mr Heerma van Voss, reproduced in: A. de Bruin, B. Hendrikx, P. Broos, et al., *Een immense vogel gelijk. Het eerste gemotoriseerde vliegtuig boven Nederland*, Maarssen 1999, 99.

2   The final bill presented to Sonneveld by Brinkman and Van der Vlugt on 26 June 1933 shows that the window was etched.

Second-floor landing with stairs to roof terrace

Stairs seen from the roof level

Rugs

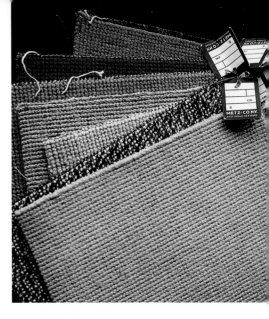

Carpet samples of bouclé carpet from Metz & Co

Rugs were laid in various rooms in The Sonneveld House, sometimes simply on top of the carpeting. One of these rugs, which was in the sitting room, has been preserved. The 3.56 x 3.60 m rug has an ecru background in which a pattern of horizontal and vertical narrow stripes and short blocks has been knotted. The rugs and other textiles in The Sonneveld House were purchased from Metz & Co. The design of this rug is still to be found in the Metz archive.[1] The archive also shows that this rug with the serial number 'S 118' was very popular and was still being sold in the 1950s.[2]

It is not known for sure who the designer was, but it may well have been Elise Djo Bourgeois, who had also designed the curtains that were hung in the kitchen. She is a likely candidate since she designed rugs for Metz and there are stylistic similarities between this one and her other textile designs.

These generally colourful, hand-knotted woollen rugs provided a warm accent in what were otherwise often severe, Modern Movement interiors designed by architects like Brinkman and Van der Vlugt. They thus function as the natural and artistic counterpart to the more anonymous, cool and industrially produced steel tubular furniture.

Like most of the other Metz rugs, this one was made in a factory in Rabat, Morocco: the Société Africaine de Filature et Tissage (SAFT). Joseph de Leeuw, director of Metz, had become a good friend of one of the directors of this Moroccan firm through his Parisian contacts. North Africa exerted a considerable influence on the applied arts in Paris in the course of the 1920s. The 'primitive' native products fitted in well with the decorative character of the ornamental designs which were popular in the French capital at the time and produced a creative impulse among many designers. Joseph de Leeuw travelled regularly through Morocco with the director of SAFT to make his own business arrangements there. For instance, he arranged for rug designs by Dutch and other European artists to be knotted in Morocco.

Besides the traditional Moroccan rugs, Metz also sold rugs designed by Bart van der Leck in the early 1930s. At the time these were one of their most modern and advanced designs. The firm also sold the slightly more conventional designs by Elise Djo Bourgeois, as well as the designs by C.A. Lion Cachet and Willem Penaat, which had become almost traditional by then. There were also smooth Moroccan rugs in colours chosen by Van der Leck, as well as the traditional Oriental, Persian and Afghan rugs. A few years later Metz also started to produce rugs with modern designs by Jean Burkhalter, Pavel Mansouroff, the architect L.C. van der Vlugt, and the young Willem Sandberg.

JC+MST

1   P. Timmer, *Metz & Co. De creatieve jaren*, Rotterdam 1995. Amsterdam Municipal Archive, Metz & Co archive, dossier 368.
2   Amsterdam Municipal Archive, Metz & Co archive, dossier 205.

Linoleum

In the 1930s it almost went without saying that the hypermodern Sonneveld House would have linoleum on the floor.[1] This product was warmly recommended at the time by all progressive interior architects. It was appreciated for its properties: waterproof, insulating, sound-absorbent, durable, odourless, and resistant to moths, dust and bacteria. This made it the ideal floor covering for kitchens, bathrooms, corridors, bedrooms and children's rooms. The functionalist architects particularly appreciated its hygienic qualities, low maintenance and its severe, light appearance.

But linoleum was reasonably expensive in the early 1930s. It was mainly hospitals and similar institutions that had it on the floor, not private homes. It was therefore a great luxury that linoleum was laid in the servants' quarters in The Sonneveld House. At first there was red linoleum in the staff rooms, but it was later replaced by black. There was beige linoleum in the servants' corridor, blue in the linen room, natural in the pantry, and grey in the guest room. The original idea was also to use a dark brown linoleum in the bedroom of Mr and Mrs Sonneveld, but in the end a more luxurious – and undoubtedly also more comfortable – dark grey woollen carpet was chosen. Linoleum was not considered suitable for the living room, where a dark brown-grey woollen carpet was laid instead. The stairs in The Sonneveld House were covered with rubber, which was even more expensive and sound-absorbent.

The linoleum for The Sonneveld House was ordered from Metz & Co in Amsterdam and was manufactured by the Nederlandsche Linoleum Fabriek Krommenie. This factory started to produce linoleum in 1899 and worked closely with factories in Scotland, Italy, France and especially Germany.[2] Linoleum was and still is made from resin, linseed oil, wood flour or cork and a colorant on a jute support. In the 1930s it was available in different thicknesses, ranging from 2 to 6 mm; the thicker it was, the more springy it was and the better it insulated. The jute came from India and East Pakistan (now Bangladesh) and was sometimes difficult to obtain. The linoleum factory was entirely dependent on this unreliable production, and so it regularly had to look for an alternative. This led to the cheap variant Linofelt, a product that was only manufactured by Krommenie. Linofelt was made of linoleum on a support of paper and tar (bitumen paper) instead of jute. A beige Linofelt was laid in the servants' corridor in The Sonneveld House. There was probably a carpet on top to muffle the sound of footsteps.

The Krommenie range of linoleum came in a variety of colours: red, green, blue, grey, various shades of brown, purple, yellow, and black. The use of cork or wood flour meant that the colours of the linoleum were never bright or really clear. Wood flour absorbs the colorant better than cork, which makes wood flour linoleum more colour-fast.

JC+MST

1 Linoleum was invented in 1863 by the British inventor Frederick Walton. He named it after the two main ingredients: flax (linum) and oil (oleum). He started the first linoleum factory in 1864. See B. Wehle Parks Snyder, 'Linoleum', *Twentieth-Century Building Materials. History and Conservation*, New York 1995, 215.

2 Interview with L. de Heer at Forbo Krommenie on 13 March 2000. See also: 'Linoleum Krommenie', *The Birth of Linoleum Krommenie*, Krommenie 1957, and J. Schoen, 'Honderd jaar linoleum in Nederland', *Met stoom* 34 (1999), 5-6.

Reconstruction of the dressing room with the original Sonneveld family furniture

Reconstruction of Puck's bedroom with original Gispen bed and cupboard interior of natural mahogany ship's joinery

Reconstruction the master bathroom
with exclusive sanitary fittings including
the ten-headed shower with chrome-
plated glass shower door, built-in bath
recess with combination tap, chrome
towel heater and console washbasins
with chrome piping

Sanitary fittings

There were no fewer than three bathrooms in The Sonneveld House: one on the ground floor for the servants, one on the second floor for the children, and another on the same floor for the parents. Each bathroom was fitted in a different way: they all had two washbasins and a bath; the family bathrooms had an additional toilet in a separate cubicle; and the parents' bathroom also had a shower. The most striking feature of the bathrooms on the second floor is the colour of the tiles and sanitary fittings – bright turquoise. The same unusual colour had been used for the tiles in the Van Nelle factory. Probably Sonneveld liked it so much there that he ordered it for his own house, but it is even more likely that they were remnants that he was able to use.

The sanitary fittings in The Sonneveld House were manufactured by Pittsburgh's Standard Sanitary Mfg. Co and were supplied by Rouppe van der Voort's industrie metaalmaatschappij, a sanitary installation company in Rotterdam. It is not known where the turquoise tiles were made or purchased.

In the early 1930s a bathroom had not yet become a standard domestic feature, let alone three bathrooms.[1] Although the price of sanitary fittings had dropped as a result of industrialised production, a fully fitted bathroom was still out of reach for many people.

It was primarily the functionalist architects who argued for a bathroom in every home – even the simplest – in the early 1930s.[2] Better hygiene and personal care would make people healthier and happier and thus more productive for society, the argument ran.

The bathrooms in The Sonneveld House were much more luxurious than most other bathrooms built at the time. Usually bathrooms contained free-standing baths, showers, washbasins, toilets and sometimes a bidet as well in plain white enamel; the walls were sometimes tiled, but they were often whitewashed, and Eternit, washable wallpaper and emulsion were also used. In The Sonneveld House the baths were built in, the boilers were out of sight, the water closets were placed not far above the toilets to reduce the noise, and the latest gadgets were included, such as a heated towel rack and a ten-nozzle shower. The comfortable and luxurious style of these bathrooms set them in the tradition of French Art Déco rather than in that of the sober Dutch version of Modern Movement.

JC+MST

1 The presence of a bath or shower was not made compulsory for all new homes in the Netherlands until 1965.

2 For insight into changing opinions in the 1920s and 1930s on hygiene in general and bathrooms in particular, see: E. Meyer, *De nieuwe huishouding* (revised by R. Lotgering-Hillebrand), Amsterdam 1931; L. Zwiers, *Ons huis. Hygiëne en gerieflijkheid*, Haarlem [1924]; J. Kloos-Reyneke van Stuwe, *Gevoelsbeschaving. Handboek voor huis en gezelschapsleven*, Rotterdam 1927; A. Bontenbal, 'Waschtafels', *Onze tuinen met huis en hof* 25 (1930), 818-819; J. Roding, *Schoon en net. Hygiëne in woning en stad*, The Hague 1986 (Architectuur en stedebouw 8), 68-69 and 75-76; W. Parent, *Sanitair. Een historisch overzicht*, Delft 1987 and K. de Leeuw, '"Schoon" zijn en gezond blijven', *Sociale Wetenschappen* 31 (1988) no. 3, 153-174.

Interior of master bedroom looking
towards the bathroom and dressing
room

Replica of Mrs Sonneveld's dressing
table, after a design by L.C. van der
Vlugt, produced by the Gispen
company

Toilet requisites

On the dressing table in the bedroom of Mr and Mrs Sonneveld stood a set of silver toilet requisites, consisting of a circular hand mirror, three different brushes, and one comb.[1] The round brush was a hair-brush, while the two longer brushes were clothes brushes: a coarser one for brushing cloaks and jackets, and a softer one for delicate fabrics such as dresses. Sets of toilet requisites never included a shoe brush – there were servants to perform that task. Unfortunately the set is not complete; all that is left of the comb is its case. Still, the tailor-made casket in which each item could be stored has survived. The lining of this casket states where the set was purchased: House of St Eloy, a well-known, exclusive jeweller in Rotterdam. It is quite likely that Mrs Sonneveld owned this set long before they moved to the Jongkindstraat.

The House of St Eloy targeted the rich Rotterdam élite of directors, bankers and shipowners, and not especially the cultural avant-garde of the day.[2] Families like Van Beuningen and Mees were among its regular customers. The jeweller's assortment consisted of silver and gold jewellery with pearls and diamonds, and silver or silver-plated objects such as candle-sticks, cutlery, sugar and cream sets, serving trays, snuff and powder boxes, tobacco jars, and cigar and cigarette boxes, often inlaid with precious tortoiseshell. Only objects made of precious metal were sold. The jewellery and other articles were manufactured by firms like Godina in Vienna and Lutz & Weiss in Pforzheim (Germany). Sometimes the owner of the House of St Eloy, A.E.M. van der Loo, commissioned objects from those firms, but the company also had its own workshop where products were designed and produced by goldsmiths employed by Van der Loo. His son and grandson also made designs and later took over the jewellery business.

Seals on the various articles belonging to the set indicate that it was manufactured in Germany. The ornamental letter V stands for 'foreign', made abroad. The butterfly represents the firm of Overbruck in Solingen, a company that went out of business long ago.[3] The House of St Eloy sold so many sets of toilet requisites that they featured as a separate item in the accounts. They were either silver-plated or solid silver, and were always sold in customised cases or caskets. Sets of toilet requisites could also be bought at De Bijenkorf and Vroom & Dreesmann, but they were usually made of less expensive and simpler materials and designed in historic styles. Mrs Sonneveld's set has a modern design, but the malleated silver gives it a traditional craft-conscious quality.

JC+MST

1 The youngest daughter Gésine also had a set of toilet requisites on her bedside table which was smoothly polished.
2 The information about the Van der Loo family and the House of St Eloy comes from an interview with Mr A. van der Loo, director of the House of St Eloy, on 14 March 2000.
3 The information about the provenance of the set of toilet requisites comes from an interview with Mr A. van der Loo, director of the House of St Eloy, on 14 March 2000.

Tabouret

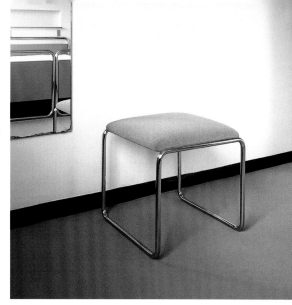

One of the many products supplied to The Sonneveld House by N.V. Gispen's Fabriek voor Metaalbewerking is a simple low stool in chrome metal with an upholstered seat, which stood in the bedrooms.[1] This product appeared in the furniture catalogue no. 52 (1933) of this Rotterdam tubular metal furniture manufacturer as 'tabouret no. 451'. It was available in different versions and at different prices.

The house also includes dozens of other Gispen chairs, armchairs and desks, even more different lamps and lamp fittings, a hat-stand and an umbrella stand. Gispen also supplied diverse accessories and interior parts, such as the special shower door, the metal house number, and the frames for the paintings.

Gispen was the obvious choice to supply furniture for the villa for a number of reasons. A few years earlier this young Rotterdam businessman had been responsible for the remarkable interior design of the Van Nelle factory, during which time Willem Gispen and Mr Sonneveld had the opportunity to get to know one another well. The ambitious owner and head designer of the furniture and lamp factory regularly worked with the architects Brinkman and Van der Vlugt, as in the case of the Van Nelle factory, but they also met more informally during club nights at De Rotterdamse Kring and at meetings of the Opbouw association of architects, of which they had been members since its foundation. Before Gispen started the large-scale production of metal furniture, the factory had already made a name for itself with its 'Gisolamps'. They were manufactured in a highly industrialised and standardised way by the late 1920s. In addition, scientific research was carried out on the most suitable type of glass for the lamp bulbs. The severe design of the fittings was the uncontroversial first choice for virtually every modern architect.

The design of the tabouret was emphatically modern, but certainly not revolutionary. This is also true of the other items of furniture that Gispen produced in the early 1930s. Other designers had preceded him in making such minimalist pieces of furniture. The basic design of the tabouret could already be seen in 1927 in Mies van der Rohe's house in the Weissenhofsiedlung in Stuttgart. Gispen lamps were also to be seen in the model homes by J.J.P. Oud and Mart Stam at this event organised by the Deutsche Werkbund.

JC+MST

1   B. Laan, A. Koch (eds) *Collectie Gispen. Meubels, lampen en archivalia in het NAi 1916-1980*, Rotterdam 1996, 73. For Gispen in General: A. Koch, *W.H. Gispen industrieel ontwerper. Een moderne eclecticus (1980-1981)*, Rotterdam 1988.

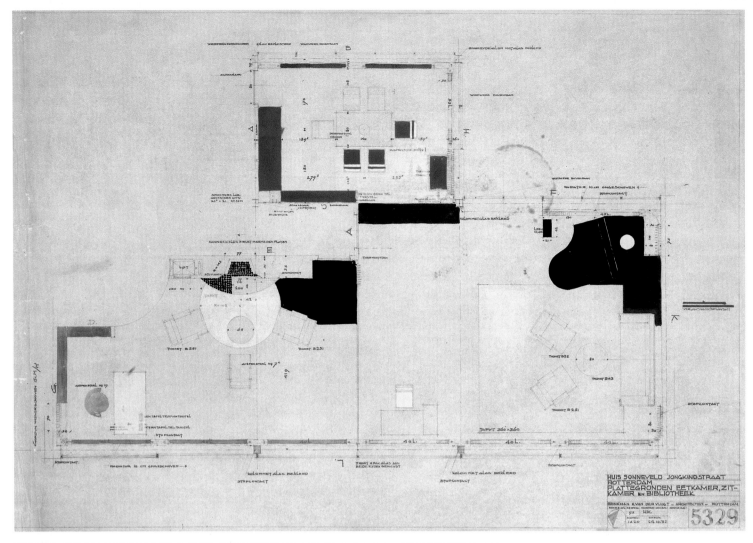

Sonneveld House, collotype of the working drawing of the living area with Thonet furniture and grand piano, 1932
Coloured with gouache

Metz & Co's fabric sample book with the Van der Leck colours that were used for upholstery, curtains, carpets and rugs

The Interior of The Sonneveld House, Then and Now

Barbara Laan and Sjoerd Wierda

An exciting exploration

The most striking thing on a first visit to The Sonneveld House was the apparently intact state of the interior, with the old washing tubs, light fittings, sanitary fittings, chrome elements and fixed furniture. Not only did the interior itself seem to have survived in an exceptionally good condition, but the other source material for an idea of what the interior of The Sonneveld House must have looked like in 1933 proved to be more varied and comprehensive than in any other case. There was a set of professional interior photographs of practically every room, which had been made within six months of the completion of the building on 17 May 1933.[1] There was a series of extremely detailed interior drawings of the main rooms from May to November 1932.[2] Moreover, the inventories of the furniture and interior fabrics, lists of the articles to be ordered, were still extant. Those lists provided an excellent insight into the pieces of furniture and sometimes even the series numbers in which they were advertised in product catalogues and the names of the fabrics and colour codes used in retail at the time.[3] The main suppliers for the interior were the Gispen company in Rotterdam for the tubular steel furniture and the light fittings, and the firm of Metz & Co in Amsterdam and The Hague for the interior textiles: the curtains, carpets, rugs, and upholstery.[4]

Nevertheless, this tremendous quantity of data was not in itself enough to be able to form a detailed and accurate picture of the interior, the colours, fabrics and other materials. The materials were only indicated in the list of fabrics by name, such as 'bouclé' for carpets, and 'Wool repp', 'épinglé', 'Peach cloth' or 'Doria velvet' for upholstery and curtain fabrics. The colours were only indicated by number, sometimes with an additional specification like 'light grey' or 'dark grey'. These rough indications covered a whole range of different shades of grey. It was also discovered that the house contained a number of later replacements and additions, so the original impression of material authenticity had to be modified.

The presence of more than two hundred colour ladders exposed all over the house by the layers of different coats of paint suggested something of the original tonal range of colours. This was merely a hint, because it is impossible to gain an impression of so many nuances in the paintwork without seeing it before you on large surfaces. In the meantime our ideas about the old upholstery and carpets began to crystallise, especially because research in the archive of Metz & Co led to the old samples and books of samples of fabrics for curtains, upholstery and carpets.[5] The luxurious quality of the textiles used in the house was surprising, but perhaps even more surprising were the colours of the fabrics. Neither did we know in advance just how wide the Metz range of fabrics was, including a separate 'colour supplement' with colours chosen by the artist Bart van der Leck.[6] This 'colour supplement' consisted of six typical Van der Leck colours: specially mixed primary colours combined with brown and two shades of grey. The range of colours was found in Peach cloth, Wool repp and several other sample books. In addition, the Forbo Krommenie linoleum factory

1   The weekly report states: 'The whole house complete except for minor activities.' Weekly report no. 48 NAI, BROX Archive d93. The date of completion was thus most likely in May 1933. By June the family was registered in the telephone directory as living in the Jongkindstraat.

2   Sketches: May-September 1931; commencement of building: 15 July 1932; interior drawings: May-November 1932; drawings of the cupboards etc. by the Allan company: December 1932. Almost the entire set of interior drawings has been preserved, except the drawing of the studio. There are two variants for two rooms: the corridor, and the youngest daughter's bedroom.

3   NAI, BROX Archive d93. The inventories of fabrics and furniture are pre-printed sheets and are dated 8 November 1932. Since the sheets were reused, this is a terminus post quem. The comments, at any rate, are later additions.

4   The starting point for the restoration and also for the 'new' interior was the situation as it was in 1933. The research on the textiles and interior on the basis of these sources was carried out by Joris Molenaar and Sjoerd Wierda for the Molenaar & Van Winden firm of architects. The follow-up research was carried out by Barbara Laan and Sjoerd Wierda for the NAI.

5   Part of the archive of Metz & Co is kept in the Amsterdam Municipal Archive, and part in the Amsterdam Historical Museum. The Amsterdam Historical Museum kindly lent the samples of textiles and carpeting required for the research.

6   Petra Timmer mentions the colours of the interior textiles, but not the type of material, neither does she show any of the types of material for the interior. She does show samples of colours on paper and samples of materials for fashion fabrics. P. Timmer, *Metz & Co. De creatieve jaren*, Rotterdam 1995, 77, 108-109.

8 November 1932.

Werk 93. Huis Sonneveld.

Meubileering en stoffeering.

	vloerbedekking	losse tapijtjes	glasgordijnen	sluitgordijnen	meubelen	meubel stof
Beg.grond Hall	grijze tegels met rand van zwart marmer	wit metalen rubber dop pen baskuleerd boulé grijs 2. (t.d lett) moet opgeven karpet en loopers	afstand 1 à 1.50 M. nader te bepalen in lacenets B.E. lichter			Peach B.4. 1 bl
Studio	Parket lichte eiken strook	2.2 lats Marokkaansne naturel moet opgeven		Doriat Velvet naturel B.4 156.		Peach B.4. bla
dienstb. kamer I	rood linoleum	rood boulé 4, het kleur in 70 × 130				Thom grijs
dienstb. kamer II	rood linoleum	rood boulé 4 het kleur in 70 × 130	Lacenets B.E. 2639 wit	Arisko cloth lichter kwak B 4 1363		
dienstgang						
1e. Verd.						
biblioth.	donker bruin boulé 17692	Marokkaansne tapijt S118 naturel	Riviera Nets Col. 52	Doria Velvet B4 145		stoeltn B.4 neure bureau B.4. 3g° bank 8
zitkamer		Marokkaansne tapijt S 118	Riviera Nets col 52	Doria Velvet B4 145 Luovlengordijne B4 156 Doria Velvet	Crapé BD 6171	Crapé BD 6 bureau B4 9 Peach
eetkamer	Boulé geel 5.	—	Riviera Nets col. 35.	Rubens Velvet B4 4052		
...dienkamer	~~rood linoleum~~ kurklinoleum naturel		Cacenets B.E. 2639 wit	Print cloth linne B.A 2312		

	vloerbedek-king	losse tapijt-jes	glasgor-dijnen	sluitgor-dijnen	meubelen	meubel-stof
...uken	tegels rood en wit	bouclé grijs 1. *een looper langs de aanrecht afmeting opgeven*	Lace nets B.E. 2639 wit.	Printed linen B.A. 2312	*bestaand taal bruin [rood] opgeven*	
verd.						
...apkr. ...ste ...hter	blauw lino-leum	bouclé N3 l. grijs Marokkaan *kleur [...] cik* 1.40 x 0.50	Riviera Neh 35	Astras Velvet B4 1051 l. grijs.		Peau-de-loche B4 903
...pkr. ...ste ...ter	blauw lino-leum grijs bouclé 1.	l. grijs Marokkaan 1.40 x 0.50 kleur v.d. cik	Riviera Neh 35	Astras Velvet B4 1051 l. grijs		Peau-de-loche B4 903
...pkr. ...n Mevr.	d. grijs bouclé 2 linoleum no. 1076	Marokkaanse naturel bij bedden en toilettafel bij deuren bouclé	Lace nets B.E. 2621	Art Canvas B4 1231		Wool Repp B4 1211 (que.)
...erkr. ...enkr.	kurk-linoleum grijs donker beige no. 1079	Marokkaanse naturel 2 stuks moet opgeven	Lace nets B.E. 2621	Mercurius Poplin NO4. Rood 143		Epingle grou B.E. 6168
				{ warenhuis gordijn { hospitaaldoek T.		
...erkr.	linoleum no. 1079 Blue Mirro Co.		Lace nets B.E. 2621. wit	Printed linen B.A. 2311.		
...r. ...n Mevr.			{ Lace nets B.E. 2639 { dubbel stel geïmpregneerd	Hospitaaldoek T.		
...dkr.	groen d. bouclé 2		Lace nets B.E. 2621	Art Canvas B4 1231	1	Wool Repp B4 1212

bouclé alm kleur / 6.50 p. M²
Marokkaanse tapijt , 30 „ „ (14x14)
        12x12 = 24
Lace nets naturel B.E. 2621 / 1.95 p. M van 1.40 M.
     listen — — „ 2.” „
     wit B.E. 2639 / 2.20 „ „
Riviera nets / 2.95 „ „ 1.30 „
Astras Velvet „ 9.25 „ 1.20 „
Astras „ „ 6.95 „ 1.20 „
Printed linen „ 5.50 „ 1.30 „
Peau cloth „ 4.95 „ 1.20 „
Epingle BD. 6171 „ 15.75 „ 1.20 „

Art Canvas / 4.95 M. 1.20 bur
Poplin 4 6 5.95 „ 180 „
     goedkooper → 3.95
Wool Repp 9.25 „ 1.30 „
Hospitaaldoek 0.95 „ 0.91 .

(Verso)

Brinkman and Van der Vlugt, List of furnishings for the Sonneveld House, 8 November 1932

Gispen desk no. 602, office chair no. 355,
desk lamp no. 403a, ceiling lights no. 168
and armchair no. 408 in the studio, 1933

Gispen furniture catalogue no. 52
(1933), hand sample book with curtain
fabrics designed by Elise Djo Bourgeois
and Gispen desk accessories on
Mr Sonneveld's desk

proved to have a book of linoleum samples from 1933
with colour codes corresponding to those used in The
Sonneveld House, yielding a virtually complete picture
of the colours of the linoleum.[7] This picture was supple-
mented by the discovery of the remains of pieces of
carpeting and above all of upholstery on the original
pieces of furniture, dozens of which turned out to be in
the possession of the family[8] – sometimes tiny scraps
of material, but often large pieces of the original upholstery fabric, sometimes with an unexpectedly bright,
unfaded rear, as on the fixed sofa in the studio.[9]

As the missing items of furniture and lamps came in
one by one, the colours returned to the walls, and the
supplies of replacement fabrics had been approved,
the picture became complete.[10] The only way to fully
experience what the interior looks like today, and the
only way to find out more or less what it must have
looked like at the time, is to see the final result of the
reconstruction with your own eyes.

Interior with tubular steel furniture

The architect Van der Vlugt was also asked to design
the interior of the house. His payment for this was in
the form of a percentage of the total sum spent on the
interior.[11] All of the furniture was to be specially purchased for the house that was to be built. In this way
the house and its interior could be designed as a whole.

The interior consisted almost entirely of steel furniture. The pieces of furniture, lamps, door and window
fittings, cupboard knobs and so on were sketched on
the interior drawings. Even the point where a clothes
hook was to be screwed into the wall was indicated.

7   The collection belongs to Forbo Krommenie bv in Assendelft. It is managed by
Mr L. de Heer. The NAI is grateful for the loan.

8   All of the items of furniture, lamps, rugs
and domestic articles that have been preserved
are collected in the Preservation of the Interior
of The Sonneveld House Foundation and were
generously loaned for the 'new' interior.

9   The research on traces of material was
conducted by textile restorer Jenny Barnett.

10   The proposal by the Collection
Department of the NAI to reconstruct the interior
in the same spirit as the exterior was shared by
the commission for the 'new' interior.

11   Declaration of fee and advance payments,
Volkskracht Historische Monumenten Collection.

The Sonneveld family with guests
in the garden, ca. 1935

The impressions of these drawings were coloured in with the colours that had been planned for the interior.

The evolution of the interior can be followed on the basis of the drawings and lists. Van der Vlugt worked with W.H. Gispen, the proprietor and chief designer of the Rotterdam company of the same name. They had already cooperated on the interior design of the Van Nelle factory, which was when the Gispen company started to manufacture tubular steel furniture. The firm had built up a good reputation since the 1920s for W.H. Gispen's progressive lamp designs.[12] Some of his designs were specially developed for the house, such as the table with a built-in electrical bell system, which has always been kept in the family. Other designs are clearly the work of Van der Vlugt, such as the impressive dressing table in the double bedroom. But most of the pieces of furniture and lamps were produced in series and could be obtained through Gispen dealers and from the Gispen showrooms.

Although there was a clear preference for the Rotterdam company, other firms were also called in and furniture designs were purchased from other artists too. For instance, pieces of furniture were ordered from the Austrian Thonet company and from the Auping firm in Deventer. Mrs Sonneveld worked at the Thonet desk B91, a design by the architect Béwé in Paris.[13] It has been preserved and now stands in the sitting room as

it did seventy years ago. Mrs Sonneveld may have simply fallen for this desk, because all the other items of Thonet furniture on the interior drawings of the living area were replaced by Gispen products.[14] It may also be that, when she was offered the choice of a Van der Vlugt design for either a desk or a dressing table, her choice fell on the latter.

The Auping firm supplied the beds for the servants' quarters and the guest room; this will have been an economy measure. The family beds were supplied by Gispen; those from the girls' rooms stayed in the family and are now back in their original position. The other beds in the reconstruction are exemplars from the period, but did not come from the family.[15]

Gispen did not supply garden furniture, so the Sonnevelds had to look elsewhere. Two of the items of garden furniture could be identified as designs by the Bauhaus designer Erich Dieckmann. They were probably supplied by the firm of Metz & Co.[16] A very similar exemplar was purchased by a gallery in Cologne.

The Sonneveld House was built between the publication dates of two Gispen catalogues, so they had to choose from catalogue 51 (1932), which was already out of date at the time. The range of tubular furniture was not very large at that moment. The 'old' models of the hat and umbrella stand, for instance, can be seen on the

Armchair model 8117 by designer
Erick Dieckmann, ca. 1932.
The Sonneveld family had two similar
chairs as garden chairs

Mrs Sonneveld in the veranda,
seated in a Dieckmann chair, 1935

interior drawing of the hall. They eventually chose the new models which appeared in catalogue 52 (1933).[17] As the armchairs in the sitting room and the library, numbers 407, 408 and 423, were first used in The Sonneveld House, it has been suggested that they were specially designed for it, but there is no hard evidence to support this hypothesis.[18] No drawings or clues pointing to the existence of these drawings have been found, so the replicas have been made on the basis of existing models and photographs. However, it is likely that this was the first time that these items of furniture were supplied by the company, as the inclusion of products in the catalogue was regularly connected with a request by a client for the production of a design. The piano lamp designed by the architect J.J.P. Oud is the best-known example of this kind.[19]

W.H. Gispen must have been familiar with the quest for suitable furniture for The Sonneveld House. A Gispen sofa without rear legs, no. 442, was first

chosen for the sitting room, a strange construction that combined three Gispen armchairs. It was included in catalogue 52. The sofa no. 441 was developed at about the same time too.

However, they eventually settled for a specially designed sofa produced by Allan & Co. It was a natural choice, as this firm was already involved in the manufacture of elements of the interior of The Sonneveld House. All of the cupboards were designed as built-in items of furniture by the firm of architects and then elaborated and produced by the interior manufacturer Allan & Co. Besides, Allan & Co had experience with comfortable upholstery for wide pieces of furniture. The company supplied railway carriage interiors at the time. Still, the decisive factor may have been an aesthetic one. The design by Brinkman and Van der Vlugt is much more balanced than the sofa that Gispen put on the market. The tubular construction that envelops the cushions, as it were, so that they cannot

12   On Gispen, his designs and the development of the factory see: A. Koch, *Industrieel ontwerper W.H. Gispen, een modern eclecticus (1890-1981)*, Rotterdam 1981.
13   P. Bromberg, *Practische woninginrichting. Een handleiding voor iedereen*, s.l. [1933], 53.
14   The Thonet armchairs were drawn in November 1932.
15   Various museums and private collectors were generous with loans and donations. Some pieces were also obtained on the market.

16   The research on the garden furniture was carried out by Otakar Máčel.
17   Most of the product catalogues of the Gispen company have been preserved. NAI, GISP 56 and 58.
18   A. Koch, 'W.H. Gispen', *Wiederhall* 14, (1993), 46, 'Leen van der Vlugt'.
19   See catalogue no. 45 in B. Laan and A. Koch (eds), *Collectie Gispen. Meubels, lampen en archivalia in het NAI 1916-1980*, Rotterdam 1996, 95-96 and the literature mentioned there.

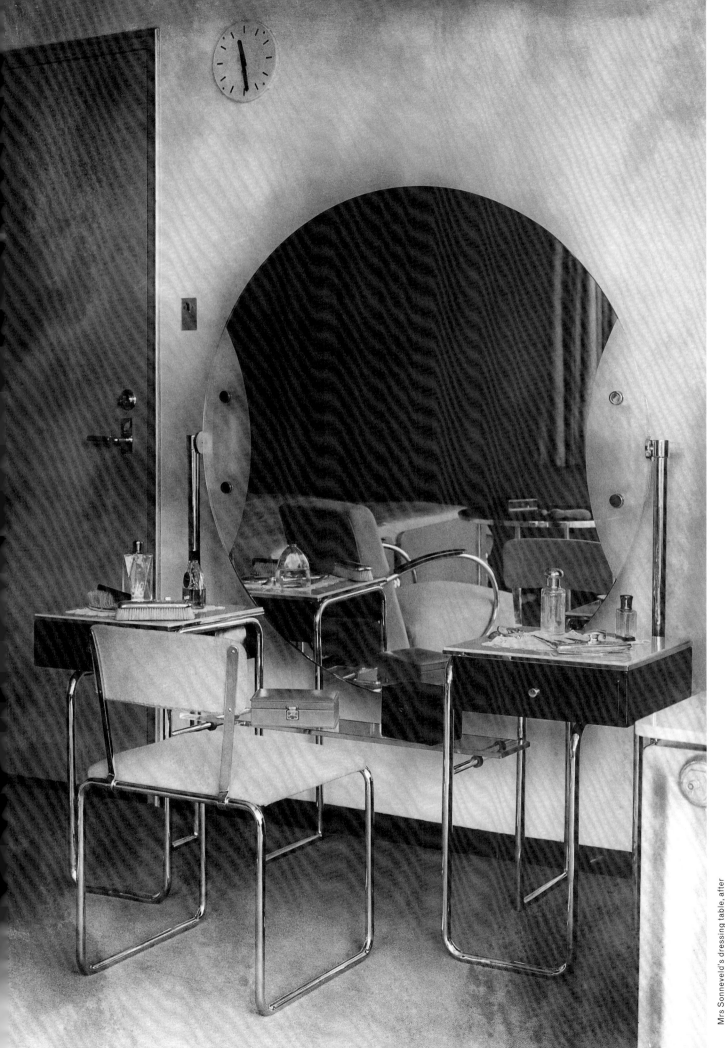

Mrs Sonneveld's dressing table, after
a design by L.C. van der Vlugt, produced by the Gispen company, 1933

Gispen wall lamp no. 312,
tabouret no. 451 and table no. 505
in the guest room, 1933

move is vaguely reminiscent of the famous armchair by Le Corbusier and Charlotte Perriand.[20] The reconstruction of the large sofa was done using the existing drawings and photographs. The small settee in the hall was also produced by the Allan company. The exemplar in the reconstructed house is the original item of furniture that remained in the family.

The design of the dressing table in The Sonneveld House goes back to an early design by Van der Vlugt which he had designed for the guest room in the house of Van der Leeuw. Both dressing tables have a large, round mirror with a single lamp behind the mirror for lighting. The one designed for the Van der Leeuw guest room is asymmetrical and has a curved table-top: the hallmark of Van der Vlugt, which betrays the influence of Le Corbusier. Since both dressing tables have disappeared, the one in the museum is a reconstruction

based on three photographs. One of these was an improvised studio photograph in the factory, and was located in the archive of the Gispen company. It shows that the dressing table was manufactured by Gispen. Another photograph shows the dressing table in situ, and this photograph too proved to be invaluable for the reconstruction because the surrounding details made it possible to deduce the dimensions. A fragment of the table can be seen in the third photograph, one of the main bedroom taken by Piet Zwart. The dressing table has been redrawn and produced as a unicum.

Many of the Gispen items of furniture for The Sonneveld House were produced with slight deviations from the standard models. For example, the dining room chairs, all six of which have been preserved, have been given arm-rests that match the shape of those on the

20 As far as we have been able to ascertain, this design did not feature in the catalogues, but it had a name: Grand Comfort, petite modèle,1928. J. van Geest and O. Máčel, *Stühle aus Stahl. Metallmöbel 1925-1940*, Cologne 1980, 72-75.

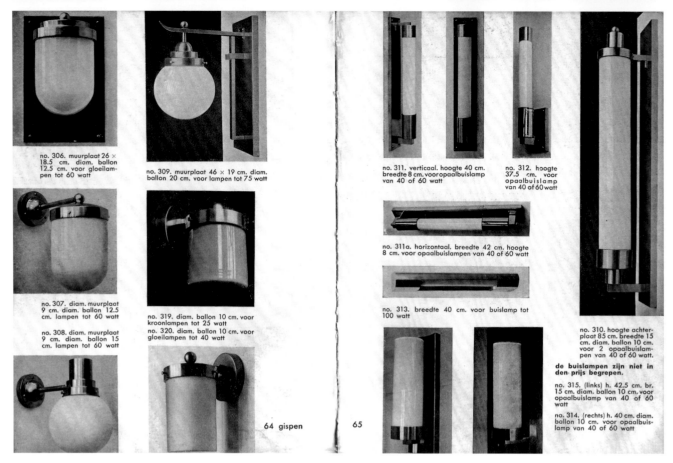

no. 306. muurplaat 26 × 18.5 cm. diam. ballon 12.5 cm. voor gloeilampen tot 60 watt

no. 309. muurplaat 46 × 19 cm. diam. ballon 20 cm. voor lampen tot 75 watt

no. 307. diam. muurplaat 9 cm. diam. ballon 12.5 cm. lampen tot 60 watt

no. 308. diam. muurplaat 9 cm. diam. ballon 15 cm. lampen tot 60 watt

no. 319. diam. ballon 10 cm. voor kroonlampen tot 25 watt

no. 320. diam. ballon 10 cm. voor gloeilampen tot 40 watt

no. 311. verticaal. hoogte 40 cm. breedte 8 cm. voor opaalbuislamp van 40 of 60 watt

no. 312. hoogte 37.5 cm. voor opaalbuislamp van 40 of 60 watt

no. 311a. horizontaal. breedte 42 cm. hoogte 8 cm. voor opaalbuislampen van 40 of 60 watt

no. 313. breedte 40 cm. voor buislamp tot 100 watt

no. 310. hoogte achterplaat 85 cm. breedte 15 cm. diam. ballon 10 cm. voor 2 opaalbuislampen van 40 of 60 watt.

de buislampen zijn niet in den prijs begrepen.

no. 315. (links) h. 42.5 cm. br. 15 cm. diam. ballon 10 cm. voor opaalbuislamp van 40 of 60 watt

no. 314. (rechts) h. 40 cm. diam. ballon 10 cm. voor opaalbuislamp van 40 of 60 watt

64 gispen   65

Gispen lamp catalogue, no. 29, 1929

armchairs in the adjacent living room. The piano stool has also been modified: it has four legs instead of the usual three. This can be seen in the exemplar that now stands in the house, which has been reconstructed using old and new components. They are slight modifications that turned the pieces of furniture in The Sonneveld House into a single family.

Lamps and fittings

Lighting was a science at the beginning of the twentieth century.[21] New lamps were developed for the optimal lighting of factories, offices and shops. Gispen was among the avant-garde designers who were experimenting with modern lighting.[22] He carried out research and produced lamps for direct and indirect light. In the 1920s he was already designing his lamps using pure geometric designs, as modern designers propagated.

The whole of The Sonneveld House was lit with Giso lamps, the name that Gispen gave to his lamps. A large number of them have survived the ravages of time and have illuminated the interior for almost seventy years. The lighting in the guest room is complete with the exception of a single wall lamp. Lamps were also kept by the family, largely because they took them with them to the later interior of the Sonneveld family in the Schiedamsevest. The glass bulbs of the Giso lamps were produced in a special way. The glass is very thin to allow plenty of light to pass through. The glass itself consists of two layers, an opal-white type of glass, and a clear type of glass. The bulbs were given a brand name of their own: 'Gisopaalglas'. Lamps fitted with these bulbs could illuminate a room just as well with a low watt lamp as their rivals could with a high watt lamp (and electricity was relatively expensive in those days).

A novelty in the interior of the house is the lighting in the library and sitting room. No fewer than twenty-two 50 cm Philinea lamps were fixed to the ceiling. The fittings resemble present-day neon lights, and have the similar quality of providing a lot of light and even lighting without shadows, but the light from these Philinea lamps is much warmer than neon light. This was due to the fact that they are not corona discharge lamps, as neon lights are, but are actually incandescent lamps with an extremely long filament. Philinea lamps are still available in different colours and sizes, so there was no difficulty in putting them back in place. Experiments with neon lighting go back at least as long as incandescent lamps. The first neon lamp for a domestic interior was presented in 1937.

Besides these batteries of lights with their high-tech look, there were lamps in the house in elementary forms like the cone, the cylinder and the sphere. Some of them are much more decorative and use a more traditional light source, such as Giso no. 63 – a lamp with an opal-white glass plate, which provided indirect lighting in the sitting room and the library. The stepped lower part of the lamp in particular is a decorative element. The no. 63 lamps that now grace the interior are replicas.[23]

The lamps reflect the same striving for uniformity as the furniture. For instance, the conical shape is a recurrent feature in the reading lamp in the library, the small lamps on the desks, and the hanging lamps in the kitchen. In the more luxurious family rooms the lamp-shades are covered with Shantung silk. The choice of lamp-shades made of fabric is a more domestic touch that looks anachronistic nowadays in such a modern interior. The same is true of the lamp in the dining room, which is inspired by the large cloth lamp-shades that used to hang above every Dutch dining table in the past. It is not surprising that this lamp was one of the best-selling Gispen lamps. Although the Gispen lamp was naturally fitted with an incandescent bulb, and there was even an opening at the bottom of the glass bowl to provide direct light above the table. In this case neither Gispen nor the Sonneveld family appear to have wanted to break with the convention of a lamp-shade made of fabric.

The colours of the artist Bart van der Leck
With the sparse furniture and the cool chrome, it is easy to forget that although this 'businesslike' interior was furnished with tubular furniture and lamps, it was also richly upholstered. The contrast between the literally cold and smooth chrome and the warm, rough upholstery on the chairs was just what appealed to the Modern Movement designers. The woolly Moroccan textiles with their warm browns and beiges were often used in modern interiors, and The Sonneveld House was no exception.

The colours in the house were in the first instance devised by the Brinkman and Van der Vlugt firm of architects. The first plan for colours in the corridors and the hall can be found in the interior drawings: doors in grey and blue, with black frames and white walls. The use of the colour blue is not fortuitous. Van der Vlugt had used the deep ultramarine blue with silver or deep blue with silver-grey in the Van Nelle factory. This use of colour was based on the standard Van Nelle colours, which were also used for company advertising. Van der Vlugt used the blue and silver(grey) in the factory offices: in the rubber on the floors, in the carpets, in the paintwork on frames and doors, in the opaque glass tops of reception desks and tables.

The second coloured drawing for the corridors is already closer to the final result: grey and soft yellow tints, frames painted in an aluminium colour, and ivory walls. A later comment on the interior drawing mentions grey with yellow, also known as champagne. The doors were eventually painted yellow and grey, but research showed that the aluminium colour was not adopted for the door frames in the corridors; they were eventually painted ivory, the colour of the walls. The frames in the hall, however, were painted in an aluminium colour, and so were most of the window frames in the house. The only other occurrence of blue in the hall was in the upholstery of the small settee there.

These modifications of the colour repertoire will have been affected, among other factors, by the choice of the upholstery selected for the house. All fabrics, carpets and other textiles were chosen from the range of the firm of Metz & Co, both from the recently published Metz books of samples for which the artist Bart van der Leck had composed the spectrum of colours, and from books for which that was not the case. The colours for the walls were probably chosen to match the colours of the curtains and upholstery, the carpet and the rugs. This seems a natural sequence, since it is easier to adapt paint to the colours of textiles that have already been dyed than vice versa. And an important clue that Van der Vlugt took into account the colours that Van der Leck had just introduced is the presence of small annotations such as 'v.d. Lek' for the grey rug in the hall, or even 'kleur van der Lek' for the rugs in the daughters' bedrooms.

21   On the development of lighting technology and fittings see: A. Koch, *Struck by lighting, an art-historical introduction to electrical lighting design for the domestic interior*, Rotterdam 1994.

22   A. Koch, *Industrieel ontwerper W.H. Gispen, een modern eclecticus (1890-1981)*, Rotterdam 1981, 50.

23   To give an impression of it, an exemplar has been taken with matt chrome and glass from EnergeticA, the museum for power technology in Amsterdam. As a result of our request, the lamp has been put into production again.

Overhead lighting with a row of
Philinea lamps in the living room and replica
of Giso hanging lamp no. 63, 2001

The bright and light colours of Bart van der Leck are present everywhere: in the colours of the carpeting, in the colours of the upholstery, and in the colours of some of the curtains. The range of colours that Bart van der Leck put together for the different Metz textiles consisted of six tints: vermilion, cornflower blue, egg-yolk yellow, dark grey, light grey, and brown. To make it easier for the customer, the advertisements stated that Van der Leck's colours were composed in such a way that you could easily combine them yourself: the carpet for the floor, the curtains for the window, the upholstery for the furniture. The idea was: Choose the fabric yourself, it will always be easy to combine the colours. The Metz & Co autumn 1931 catalogue contained the following entry:[24]

> SUNFIRM FABRICS, IN COLOURS BY PAINTER B. VAN DER LECK.
>
> It seemed to us that there was a great demand for these modern colours, so we decided to maintain this range of colours in different qualities.
> This makes it possible to use these colours that are so suitable in modern interiors for many purposes.
> In choosing this range of colours, the painter's intention was that these fabrics should form a good colour combination when used for curtains, upholstery, cushions, etc.
>
> WE CURRENTLY STOCK THESE V.D. LECK COLOURS IN THE FOLLOWING QUALITIES:
>
> SUNFIRM PEACH CLOTH highly suitable for curtains, upholstery, cushions, etc.
> 130 cm wide, ƒ 5.95 per metre
> SUNFIRM RUBENS VELVET heavy velvet for upholstery and curtains
> 130 cm wide, ƒ 7.75 per metre
> SUNFIRM LINEN, heavy course-threaded linen for curtains, coverings, etc.
> 130 cm wide, ƒ 3.95 per metre
> WOOL REPP a strong woollen repp material for upholstery
> 130 cm wide, ƒ 9.25 per metre
> LANA SERGE our familiar heavy woollen serge for divan covers and tablecloths
> 130 cm wide, ƒ 5.50 per metre

'Peach cloth', a luxurious raised cotton, better known by the name of 'peau de pêche', was chosen for the upholstery of the armchairs in the library (vermilion), the office chairs in the daughters' studio (vermilion and cornflower blue), Mrs Sonneveld's office chair in the sitting room (egg-yolk yellow), and the small settee in the hall (cornflower blue). The same material in black was used for the dining room chairs and for Mr Sonne-veld's office chair in the library. A black peau de pêche is still made today, but it was necessary to have the Van der Leck tints specially made because they are no longer available.

'Rubens velvet' was also used for curtains in The Sonneveld House in the dining room (blue) and in the daughters' bedrooms (light grey).

'Wool repp' is also to be found on the list of fabrics. It was used for the upholstery of the fixed sofa in the studio. Traces of material that were found beneath various other fabrics for the upholstery of this sofa confirm that it was a cornflower blue raised corduroy with thin cotton chain threads and a thick woollen weft which give the fabric a rough appearance.[25] The list indicates that a yellow Wool repp was also used in the house. This was on the armchairs of the sitting area of the bedroom of Mr and Mrs Sonneveld. Unfortunately the colour number does not correspond to the two tints of yellow that were found in the sample book, so that the right shade of colour had to be guessed for the reconstruction. Wool repp is not made any more, but it proved possible to find a woollen fabric with the same cord and rough texture.

The samples of woven bouclé carpeting that were found in the Metz archive did not have names or colour numbers. The mention of the colour numbers 1 to 5 on the list of upholstery with the annotations light grey 1, dark grey 2, red 4, blue 3, and yellow 5, make it very likely that Bart van der Leck tints were used here too.[26] The colours in the sample books matched the Van der Leck colours in the other ranges of fabrics. These colours were therefore chosen for the woollen bouclé that was specially woven in this colour and can now be seen in various rooms in The Sonneveld House. The bouclé carpets had to be specially woven for the house, particularly because the Van der Leck tints are no longer available.

Research on the curtains in the kitchen, service room and linen room has shown that chequered curtains designed by Elise Djo Bourgeois were hung in these rooms. It is a hand-printed linen. Using silkscreen technique, it was relatively easy to reconstruct the original pattern in the right shades: yellow and grey for the service and linen room, red and grey for the kitchen.

The curtains that were hung in front of the largest windows in the house were made of a chenille called 'Doria velvet'. The fabric is soft and rather loose as a result of the chenille thread, a thread that seems to be laced, as it were, by the short and fluffy threads of a secondary warp. Since chenille is a double-sided textile, the curtains also present a sumptuous front to the outside world. The chenille found in the sample book in the Metz archive is a supple cotton fabric with a fairly open pile. The open pile makes it look like a fabric with thin, horizontal stripes. The chenille that hangs in front of the windows of the studio and living room today is made of cotton, but lacks these stripes.

MAUSER

STAHL-MÖBEL

MAUSER WERKE
WALDECK G.M.B.H.
WALDECK
(BEZ. KASSEL)

Reproduction from a brochure of
Mauser cupboards, as originally
installed in the kitchen of the
Sonneveld House

The upholstery of the furniture in the sitting area, however, is striped. The striped effect of the épinglé could be clearly seen in photographs. In the case of the sofa in particular it afforded a welcome vertical interruption of its large backrest. The beige tint that it now has matches the browns, beiges and ivories from the immediate surroundings: the natural colours of the rug that was made after the original, the chenille curtains in a brown tint that was known from the sample book, and the bronze-coloured brown of the walls. Oral tradition has it that the colour was 'sandy', but we shall never know whether this sandy colour was closer to beige or to yellow.

A striking feature of the way in which the colours for the upholstery were chosen is that, if they were in a Van der Leck colour, they usually created (colour) accents with regard to their immediate surroundings. This is true of the yellow of Mrs Sonneveld's office chair and of the office chairs of her daughters, as well as of the armchairs beside the fireplace. In the dining room, however, which was conceived in Van der Leck colours as systematically as the daughters' bedrooms were, the upholstery works in the opposite way.[27] Here the colours are used for the large surfaces: red for the dining room cupboards, blue for the curtains and yellow for the floor, while the table and chairs present a combination of their natural colour with black, grey and chrome.

An interesting aspect of the interior of The Sonneveld House is that it seems to be an early – perhaps even the earliest – example of an interior with Van der Leck fabrics. The living area in The Sonneveld House seems to have been deliberately kept free of the bright primary colours. The atmosphere of the space is determined by brown: the brown of the Doria velvet and the bronze-brown walls in harmony with it, a dark brown carpet, and the hand-made rug. But it has its surprising colour accents too: the bright yellow of Mrs Sonneveld's office chair and the orange-red in the sitting area near the hearth: both upholstered in Peach cloth in the Van der Leck tints.

How authentic is the new interior?

An attempt has been made to reconstruct the complete interior of The Sonneveld House in its original colours so that the house could be opened to the general public as a museum. The decision to show how people lived in 1933 to the museum public was connected with an appreciation of this unique *Gesamtkunstwerk* by Brinkman and Van der Vlugt.[28] Each of the individual rooms, the colour surfaces that have been given a place there, and the elements of the interior that occupy a place there, have been combined to form a balanced composition of space, colour and volume. Every room, every corner and every area has several horizontal and vertical colour borders and contains several three-dimensional objects which are absorbed by it or stand out from it through a colour accent. The colour surfaces and colour accents are not isolated elements, but they confer meaning on a wall, an area or a piece of furniture. That meaning is functional in the sense that it is connected with the manner of use: pillar-box red stands for 'service', bronze-brown is literally the background colour, the décor, for Mr and Mrs Sonneveld.

24 Amsterdam Municipal Archive, Metz & Co Archive 488.

25 Colours that cropped up and differed from the extant list are the sofa in the studio and the vermilion office chair, in combination with grey and light orange-yellow in the paintwork.

26 The brown bouclé was numbered 17692, and was thus probably not a Van der Leck colour.

27 In the daughters' bedrooms the Van der Leck colours were used for the carpet, the bedside rug, the upholstery and the curtains.

28 The major exception to the rule is the retention of the standard kitchen element that Piet Zwart designed for Bruynzeel and that was put into production in 1937. That Bruynzeel kitchen unit can still be admired today in the kitchen of The Sonneveld House because of its historical value. It is not known why the original steel Mauser kitchen cupboards were replaced at an early stage by the present wooden kitchen cupboards from Bruynzeel. They have been left as they are because they were introduced by the family itself and because they were in a good condition, even though they are actually an anachronism in the whole.

The interior design can best be characterised as a harmonious composition in which both Van der Vlugt and (indirectly) Van der Leck had an important share.[29] Often only one wall is coloured, like the bronze-brown wall in the Sonnevelds' bedroom, or a part of the wall marks how the area is used, like the light-blue colour field that marks the corner where the bed is situated in the eldest daughter's bedroom. In the enormous living area the colour surfaces put a stop to a feeling of being lost. They lend a helping hand, and what is more important: they define an area, so that how a corner or part of the space is used is made immediately clear.

The interior that Bart van der Leck himself designed for the branch of Metz & Co in The Hague, using the fabrics that he had designed, was completed in 1934, soon after The Sonneveld House. The colour scheme here is comparable in its use of colour and materials, but it goes further in abstracting colour surfaces so that the space is subordinated to the use of colour, which is nowhere the case in The Sonneveld House.

Van der Vlugt also made use of the 'ton sur ton' principle. The effect of this use of colour, in which (often in frames and adjacent surfaces) colours are used that are only a shade different from one another, yields an exceptionally rich and varied total picture. It is as if a three-dimensional quality – the quality of shadow, or at least its semblance – is conferred on a two-dimensional technique – painting. It is known that 'ton sur ton' was very popular in the last quarter of the nineteenth century. It considerably enlivens an interior because it accentuates the shadow effect of frames and surfaces.

Although an important value lies in the total impression of colours and materials that have been thought out down to the tiniest details, the principle of trying to achieve maximal visual authenticity that has been followed in The Sonneveld House is itself, of course, open to question. After all, the use of paint and the interior textiles are new and close to the situation in the year 1933, but the material itself is not authentic. On the other hand, the original mirrors and chrome layers have been respected as much as possible, although it is easy to replace them both. The degree to which original pieces of furniture and lamps could be replaced in their original position has affected the reticence which has also been adopted as a conservation principle with regard to the semi-fixed elements of the house.[30]

The degree of authenticity of the interior is deceptive. Roughly two-third of the original furniture once stood in this house; the rest is original and taken from somewhere else, or new. Of course, it would have been possible to replace only the family possessions in the house, but that would have created a lack of proportion between furnished and unfurnished parts of the house. Besides, the picture would not have been complete. Given the original intention of furnishing the house with items of furniture and lamps that were produced in series, it seemed legitimate to try to find the series numbers that are no longer among the family's possessions. The replicas of the large sofa, the armchairs in the living area, the desks of the Sonneveld daughters, the dressing table, the tea table, the kitchen table and several lamps fill the remaining gaps. So completeness predominates over the impression of the authenticity of each individual item.

How close the newly produced items of furniture are to the originals varies from one case to another and is heavily dependent on the documentation that has been preserved. Sometimes there was only a black and white photograph, as in the case of the dressing table, while in other cases the original exemplar was still in existence, such as the living room rug, that was too fragile to be put on show.

The difference between 'authentic and fake', 'old and new', 'then and now', turns out in the end to be a relative one. After all, the reconstruction has led to so many new insights into The Sonneveld House in particular and into the Dutch Functionalist movement in general that the work that has gone into it has been worthwhile in every way. Besides, a reconstruction is actually the only way to obtain a complete visualisation of an interior.

29   It is unlikely that Van der Vlugt and Van der Leck had any contact on the design of the interior of The Sonneveld House. Neither the Brinkman and Van der Vlugt and Metz & Co archives nor the archival material of Bart van der Leck contain anything to support such a hypothesis. We are grateful for information about the Metz archive to Petra Timmer, and about the Bart van der Leck archive to Cees Hilhorst.

30   The Collection Department of the NAI took the lead in research on the core materials and finishing layers of the metal pieces of furniture, lamps, balustrade, door knobs, window fittings, cupboard knobs, cover plates, screws, curtain rails, sanitary fittings, decorative borders, etc. Only the furniture and door knobs turned out to be made of iron; the other elements (more than a thousand) are made of brass. The technical research was carried out by the Netherlands Institute for Cultural Heritage (ICN). Two metal restorers, Joostje van Bennekom and Suzanne Meijer, devised the appropriate methods of treatment for the conservation of all this shiny chrome material.

Detail of the front door of
The Sonneveld House, 2001

Research using colour 'ladders', 1999
Molenaar & Van Winden

Photomicrograph of a colour sample
Sikkens / AKZO coatings
Sassenheim

Reconstruction of an Atmospheric Colour Scheme

Lisette Kappers and Joris Molenaar

The colour scheme of the interior of The Sonneveld House comes as a surprise. A rich palette of colours could be expected on the basis of the archival material and the comments by architect Jaap Bakema (see p. 65) and others. Nevertheless, one tends to expect a Modern Movement interior to be predominantly white and silver-grey with accents in primary colours. The interiors by Brinkman and Van der Vlugt with their many ochres, the absence of pure white, and the use of blue, yellow and red tints that are never harsh and full, but are subdued and in harmony with the surrounding fabrics and furniture, have to be seen for their surprising effect. Everything seems to fit together so naturally that it is astonishing how much research it has taken to arrive at this result.

Sources

At the start of the restoration there were no traces left of the original colour scheme except for the colours of materials such as black marble, tiling and opaque glass window-sills. The house had been repainted in dazzling white by the last occupants: all of the woodwork and the spiral staircase had been painted bright yellow. That was where the quest for the original colour scheme started. Close examination of the original black and white photographs makes it possible to distinguish colour nuances, gloss and surface structure, but not to determine them with precision. The metal gloss of the bronze-coloured and aluminium-coloured paints can be seen clearly in the photographic material. It is also possible to distinguish upholstery and furniture finishings, and to draw up a preliminary, general range of colours on the basis of the indications on coloured working plans and samples of upholstery and furnishings. Nevertheless, the medium of black and white photography is still too abstract to convey the atmosphere of the colour scheme that was actually used.

Statements by members of the family and relatives who knew the house in its original state also provided several clues, but the recollection of colour is an extremely subjective question, and its reliability can vary considerably from one person to another.

Of course, the most important source of information for the investigation was the house itself. The original coat of paint was still present beneath the many coats that had been applied later to the walls, ceilings, window-frames, doors and fixed furniture. A regular way of tracing this information is to perform a 'paint scratch' (mechanical research). The resulting 'colour ladders' shows every coat of paint, from the first primer to the latest layer. Layer by layer, samples of the paint are removed using a scalpel. Each sample represents a deeper layer, so that eventually a strip is created that exposes every coat of paint as in an archaeological excavation. More than two hundred of such ladders were scratched in The Sonneveld House.

The next stage is to determine the original finishing coat for each ladder. This calls for working in an extremely critical way and for confirmatory evidence each time. Especially in the case of painting, it can happen that, while work is going on, an experiment is made and a different colour is then chosen. Some of these choices were indicated on the colour plans that Brinkman and Van der Vlugt made for each room, but not every change was recorded at the time.

The studio walls puzzled us in this way. Some walls had first been painted turquoise, while others were decorated with a grey stippled emulsion. However, this coat of paint was also found as a second coat on top of the turquoise. Was the turquoise coat an experiment that did not find acceptance, or was it used and the decision to repaint these walls taken at a later date? This question could be answered in the laboratory by investigation of the composition of the paint and the way in which one coat of paint adhered to the other. As there were no traces of dirt between the different coats and they adhered excellently, it was concluded that the turquoise must have been covered by another layer of paint right away and thus that the walls must have been grey when the house was completed. The bold turquoise has therefore not been replaced in the restoration in order to preserve the authenticity.

Research on colours and materials

By using all of the available sources, making systematic analyses and carrying out comparisons, it proved possible to determine the original coating in the ladder in most cases. In case of doubt the laboratories of the Akzo Coatings company with support of the Sikkens Foundations or the Netherlands Institute for Cultural Heritage (ICN) were called in. Microscopic investigation enabled identification of the right layers and analysis of the composition of the paints. For this purpose a sample was taken from the object of analysis. This cross-section through all the coats of paint down to the primer was then covered with resin, polished, and examined through the microscope. This clarified the sequence of coats of paint and layers of dirt, enabling identification of the right layer of paint. Various samples were also compared with one another in order to determine similarities on the basis of composition. This proved to be a highly suitable method for determining in particular how many tints of beige and grey had been used.

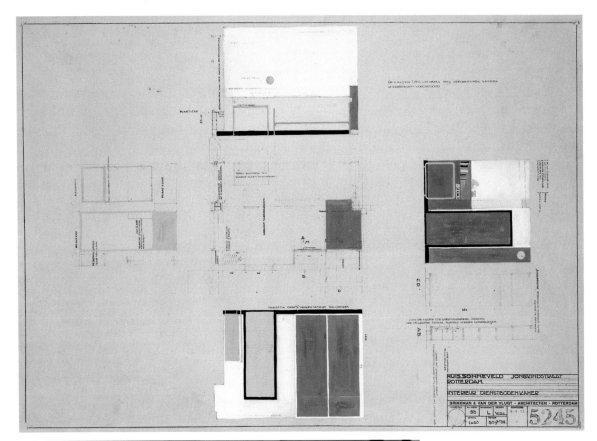

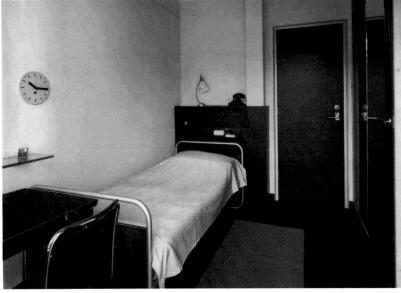

Example of the first colour group:
Working drawing no. 5245, 30 July 1932
Interior servants' room
Tracing coloured with poster paint

Example of the first colour group:
Interior of the servants' rooms
Coloured black and white photograph
Photograph: Jan Kamman 1933,
edited by Molenaar & Van Winden

The bedroom of Mr and Mrs Sonneveld, looking towards the bathroom
Coloured black and white photograph
Photograph: Piet Zwart, 1933, edited by Molenaar & Van Winden

In a few cases it was decided to carry out pigment investigation and an EDX analysis. The proportions of different pigments in the paint determine its colour. This is the purest, but also the most time-consuming way of reconstructing a colour. The EDX method of analysis enables comparisons between the components of the different coats of paint.

After the original paint layer had been determined, the following step was to gauge the colour. Since paint changes colour even when it is not exposed to light, it was necessary to expose the original colour on the colour ladder to daylight for a time. In many cases it proved impossible to reconstruct the original colours using present-day colour recipes. The AAC codes of the present-day Sikkens range of colours were used to determine the colour precisely. Those codes were sought which corresponded the closest to the original colour. On the basis of this rough indication, the painter mixed the colours on the spot until the original colour of the ladder had been found.

Besides colour, the original degree of gloss and surface structure also determine the authenticity of the reconstruction. Five different types of paint were used by Brinkman and Van der Vlugt in the interior of The Sonneveld House. They were applied again during the restoration. Doors, woodwork and radiators were delivered on the spot pre-varnished, according to the provisions of the list of specifications. They were then finished with an oil-based silky matt emulsion. The mahogany and okoume woodwork on the inside of the cupboards was stained and finished with neutral boat varnish where necessary. The walls and ceilings of the living area were finished with a stippled emulsion with a very fine structure which was applied to a completely smooth, prepared Swiss muslin. The walls of the service rooms and bathrooms were treated with an Amstelline masonry paint with an aluminium-colour

metal paint on the steel frames, while the steel frames, radiators and several parts of the walls in the living room, library and the parents' bedroom were finished in a sprayed bronze colour.

In order to determine the precise surface structure and degree of gloss, the restoration work included a search for places where the original surface of a final coat of paint could be exposed. A few panels that had never been repainted served as a point of reference for the varnishes. It was easy to expose the surface of the stippled walls because the later coats of paint did not adhere well. The fineness of the structure could be checked on patches behind the lamps which had never been repainted. The original metal gloss of the bronze-coloured and aluminium-coloured paint was found on the rear of radiators that had never been repainted. In particular, the silky gloss stippled walls and the metal gloss produced a special effect in the interior that is very different from the coats of latex and cement paint that were applied later.

To preserve this information, it was decided to spare the old layers of paint by applying a new, extremely smooth primer on top of them in the restoration. This primer has then been covered by emulsions in as authentic and pure a finish as possible in the original colour and texture.

Colour schemes

Three kinds of colour schemes can be distinguished on the basis of the results of the detailed colour investigation in The Sonneveld House. The first group of colours was used in the service rooms, corridors and passages, which are entirely in beige tints. In the service areas the beige matches the colour of the tiling, with only the addition of a deep red accent on doors and furniture. The hall, staircase and corridors have light-yellow accents on doors leading to rooms, and green-grey on cupboard doors and radiators against walls in a beige finish with a light pink tinge.

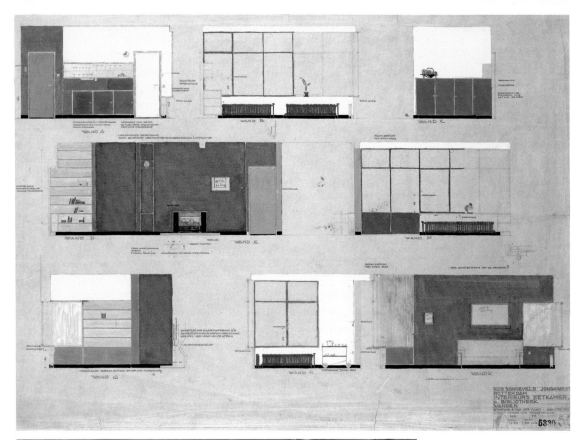

Example of the second colour group:
interior of the living room and library
Working drawing no. 5330,
24 October 1932
Tracing coloured with poster paint

Example of the second colour group:
interior of the living room and library
Coloured black and white photograph
Photograph: Piet Zwart 1933,
edited by Molenaar & Van Winden

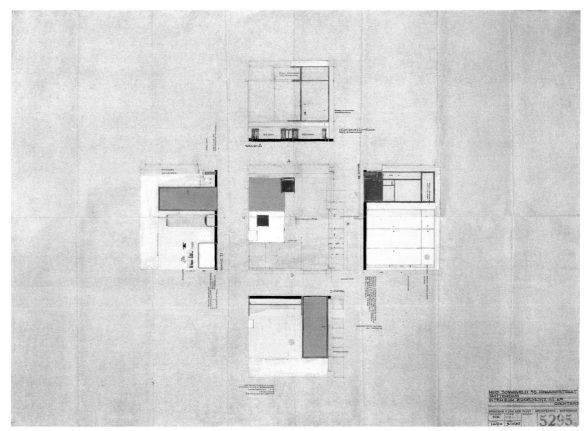

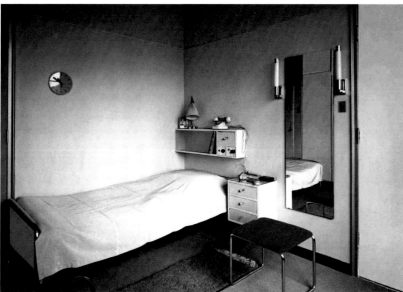

Example of the third colour group:
interior of the daughter's bedroom
on the south side of the house
Working drawing no. 5295,
3 October 1932
Tracing coloured with poster paint

Example of the third colour group:
interior of the daughter's bedroom
on the south side of the house
Coloured black and white photograph
Photograph: Jan Kamman 1933,
edited by Molenaar & Van Winden

The second group of colours was used in the rooms where the Sonnevelds lived and received their guests. This group consists of ochres, bronze, brown and beige tints, with the addition of the occasional colour accent in the furniture, such as light yellow in the parents' bedroom or vermilion by the fireside in the study. The application of a bronze-coloured metal gloss on the walls, radiators and steel window-frames in these rooms is striking, especially as a background for the seating and resting areas.

A third group of colours can be found in those rooms where subdued tints of red, yellow and blue were used for the fixed furniture and the upholstery, such as in the studio for the daughters, the dining area, or the daughters' bedrooms.

The upholstery and other fabrics are taken from the collection of the firm of Metz & Co that the artist Bart van der Leck had put together as a colour consultant. The colour accents applied on the walls and woodwork in these rooms are the pastel versions of De Stijl colours which are so characteristic of this artist.

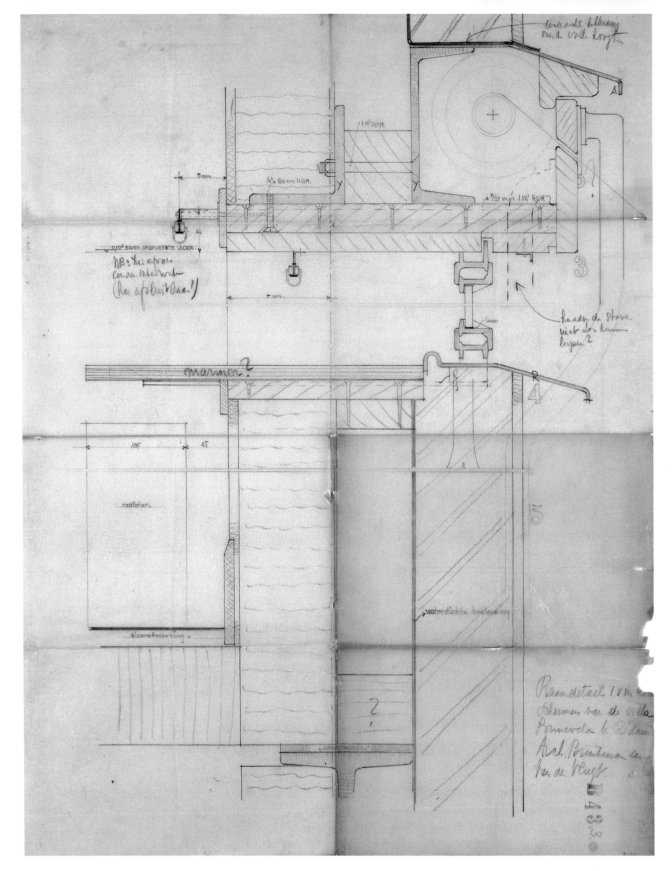

Detail sketch of the windows in
the west wall, Brinkman and
Van der Vlugt, 1932

A Modern Villa from 1933 in 2001 'As if nothing has happened'

Willem Jan Paijmans and Joris Molenaar

The preservation of the authentic Sonneveld House, designed by Brinkman and Van der Vlugt, as an important part of the Rotterdam cultural heritage, was the direct motivation for the purchase of these premises (12 Jongkindstraat) by the Stichting Volkskracht Historische Monumenten. The house only changed hands a few times in more than 65 years. The original fabrics and furniture were taken by the Sonnevelds in 1954 when they furnished the apartment at no. 140 Schiedamsevest in Rotterdam where they spent their retirement. After serving for more than twenty-five years as the official residence of the Belgian consul in Rotterdam, this monumental house was acquired by Volkskracht in 1997. As the consul's family lived mainly in Belgium and the Belgian state had not provided a large budget for the adaptation of the residence, the maintenance of the house after the departure of the Sonneveld family was still aimed at conservation. This took place in a manner that delayed and disguised rather

than combatted the technical problems. As a result, much of the original interior and furnishing of the house has remained intact, such as tiling and sanitary appliances, rubber carpeting and a great deal of chrome metalwork and light fittings. The garden, an essential décor for this urban villa in the heart of Rotterdam, was neglected and subsided more and more. The low garden fence was replaced by a tall one with a conifer hedge, so that the open garden was turned into a mysterious and inaccessible enclave in the city. What at first sight seemed to be a question of overdue maintenance for this young historic building turned out after detailed study to call for drastic restoration.

Aim of the restoration in relation to the aims of Volkskracht and the Netherlands Architecture Institute

After the purchase of the house, the office of Molenaar & Van Winden architecten in Delft was invited to make an inventory and description of the technical state of The Sonneveld House in the middle of 1997. The purpose of this was to determine the authenticity of the state of the house at that time.[1] The Stichting Volkskracht Historische Monumenten acquires objects, restores them and makes them suitable for an appropriate new function. In determining this new function, priority is given to the value of the monument, its continued existence is guaranteed, and a cultural purpose can be served by opening it to the general public. After Volkskracht had decided to collaborate with the Netherlands Architecture Institute on the reuse and management of the house, a commission was set up to supervise the restoration of the exterior and interior.[2] The information collected at the inventory stage made

[1] At Molenaar & Van Winden architecten, Joris Molenaar was the architect responsible for the restoration. Preparatory work for the project was carried out by Willem van der Bas, Lisette Kappers, Willem Jan Paijmans (project manager) and Sjoerd Wierda. Close collaboration took place with the Collection Department of the Netherlands Architecture Institute, conservator and project manager Barbara Laan, Sjoerd Wierda and others.

[2] The members of the commission: prof. W.H. Crouwel (chairman), on behalf of the Stichting Volkskracht Historische Monumenten: J. van der Leeuw, J. Boot, on behalf of the Netherlands Architecture Institute: M. Willlinge (head of the Collection Department) and B. Laan (conservator and project manager Sonneveld), on behalf of Molenaar & Van Winden architecten: J. Molenaar.

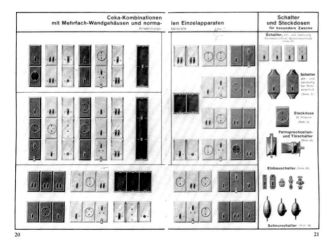

Reproduction from a Siemens brochure of electric switches as originally installed in the Sonneveld House

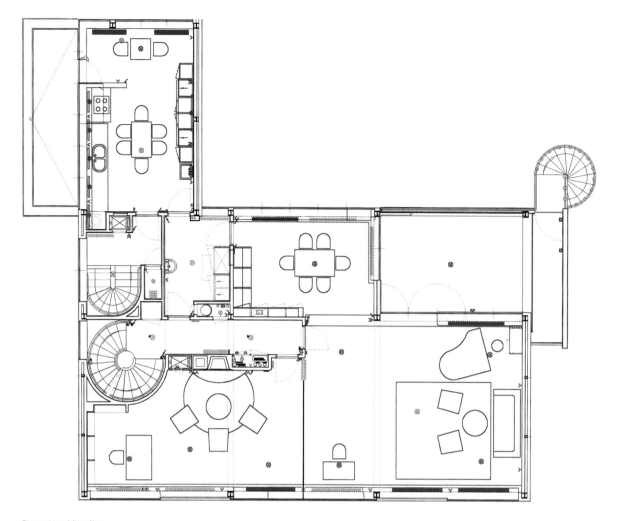

Floor plan of first floor,
inventory sketch,
September 1998
Molenaar & Van Winden

it possible to reconstruct as comprehensive as possible a picture of the original house, including the interior and furnishing. The debate on the restoration and new function led to the conviction that the implementation of a complete reconstruction of the original house, including the garden, the interior and the furniture, was preferable to restoring only the outside and fitting out the interior for exhibitions of design classics, for example. It was therefore decided not to restore The Sonneveld House with a view to a totally different function, but to reconstruct it in its original 1933 state as if nothing had happened in the meantime, and then to exhibit it to the general public as a collection item by the Netherlands Architecture Institute. The choices made during restoration are all based on this principle. A sound reconstruction called for further investigation in and of the house.

1997, the house stripped bare
Everything that was found in The Sonneveld House was described at the beginning of the inventory and labelled as original or as a later addition. The informa-

tion contained in old building plans was used to produce new computer drawings on which the findings were then incorporated.[3] The next stage was to compile room-by-room lists of the interior furnishings with data on the colour scheme, lighting, furniture, upholstery and fabrics where the Brinkman and Van der Vlugt archive allowed.[4] However, the jigsaw puzzle that all this information yielded was still too incomplete to be able to reconstruct a fully authentic picture on the base of it.[5] The missing information had to be obtained from investigation carried out in the house itself. As a preparatory stage for the restoration and reconstruction, a search for clues in and around the house was begun and continued during the restoration: the house itself was made the starting-point.[6]

It was discovered that a major renovation of the premises had taken place in the early 1980s, during which the steel frames in the west wall elevation had unfortunately been replaced by aluminium ones from the building trade, the original balustrades and the windbreak had been removed from the roof, the roof terraces had been covered with roofing material, and

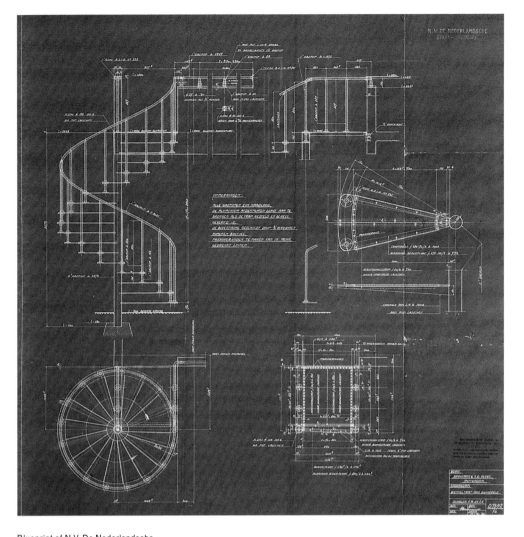

Blueprint of N.V. De Nederlandsche
Staalindustrie of the working
drawing for the steel spiral staircase
of the veranda

a few changes had been made to technical details which
had a negative effect with regard to damp. The original
garage doors and the low steel garden fence had been
replaced. In the interior the authentic atmosphere had
been gradually expelled by the introduction of curtain
coves that did not match the house, radiator cupboards
and deep pile fabrics in neutral colours, culminating in
the painting of everything in white and yellow. Defects
in the luxurious sanitary fittings, the introduction of
discordant electric switches, the freezing of irreplace-
able cast-iron radiators and the recent demolition of
the original kitchen fittings had serious effects on the
originally fairly complete technical installations. The
steel window frames that remained manifested the
predictable defects, and the original built-in awnings
above them had all fallen into disuse or had even been

removed. Ugly shutters and security lamps had been
screwed to the outside walls, and the veranda had
been turned into a cage through the addition of slidable
steel lattice-work. The plastered and whitewashed
façades betrayed the existence of many repairs and
could not disguise the fact that the steel construction
behind them had started to rust. The tiling indoors and
outdoors had been partly damaged or removed during
maintenance work, as had the opaque glass casing of
the columns and window-sills.

Source research
The preparations for restoration and reconstruction
yielded much information about the building technology, architectural details and interior design of The
Sonneveld House. In reconstructing the original state,

3   This work was carried out by Willem van
der Bas in close consultation with the author.
4   This interior research was carried out by
Sjoerd Wierda and Willem van der Bas in close
consultation with the author.
5   The reconstruction of the interior is a joint
project of the Collection Department of the
Netherlands Architecture Institute and Molenaar &

Van Winden architecten. For detailed information
see the list of those involved on the inside cover
6   On this see: Joris Molenaar, 'Huis
Sonneveld. Bron van atmosferische nieuw-
zake-lijke interieurkunst', in: *Jaarboek Cuypersgenootschap 2000. Achter geloten deuren.
Bronnen voor interieurhistorisch onderzoek*, 16
(2001), 70-83.

however, the object itself cannot serve as the only source. Verification of facts and counterarguments are necessary in the discussions on what the authentic state was, in order to decide on the most reliable and comprehensive plan of reconstruction. Additional information from sketches and from written and oral sources is essential.

A lot has been preserved in the Brinkman and Van der Vlugt archive, but fate has limited the amount of information available, for almost half of the archive, which was stored in a cellar in the part of Rotterdam outside the dikes, was lost in the flood of 1953. In some cases the surviving parts of the archive have suffered serious damage from water. Almost all of the design drawings for The Sonneveld House are still extant. Lists of specifications and construction data are incomplete because most of the contract drawings, working drawings and detail drawings have been lost. However, there are impressions of a number of drawings with remarks on the installations, for example, or the fixed furniture. There are also blueprints from the suppliers of the steel frames, the steel fences and the outdoor staircase, the fixed furniture and various technical installations. In the case of The Sonneveld House, then, it is precisely the information on details

that has been obtained from investigation and taking measurements in the house itself, while an analogy could sometimes be made with information on the houses designed by Brinkman and Van der Vlugt for De Bruyn and Boevé.

Analysis of the design and technical elaboration
The search for the internal logic of the house offers arguments for choices: a protection against excessive speculation in decision-making. Otherwise there is a high risk that choices will be made with arguments like: 'this is what Van der Vlugt preferred', or 'if Brinkman and Van der Vlugt had been alive today they would have done it like this', or 'this must be a compromise between the architect and the client, because it is at odds with the current theory about the architecture of Brinkman and Van der Vlugt'. Through a study of the design process, the restoration architect gains more insight into the functional, spatial and organisational logic of the house and a feeling for the compositional characteristics of the monument. This means that decisions can be backed up with arguments when it comes to drawing up the plan of restoration. At a later stage of the implementation too, this insight serves as a guide for changing the activities where necessary.

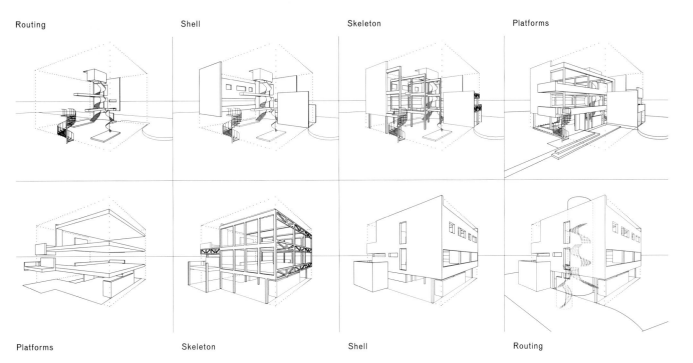

Routing   Shell   Skeleton   Platforms

Platforms   Skeleton   Shell   Routing

Analysis of Sonneveld House,
Willem van der Bas and Joris Molenaar
Molenaar & Van Winden
Top: seen from the south-east
Bottom: seen from the north-west

The restoration architect has to base his actions on the facts of his study object and the results of the analyses to which he subjects it. In the case of subjects for which the necessary information is lacking, he has to be able to develop the arguments himself from his specialised knowledge of the object itself instead of justifying his choices mainly with generalities about the architecture in question.

The Sonneveld House was built using a wide variety of materials, constructions and installations. The main supporting structure consists of a skeleton of steel columns and beams fastened with rivets. They support the floors, which are made of steel bridging joists with prefabricated light concrete plates. This skeleton stands on a foundation of reinforced concrete resting on driven piles. This basement is partly arranged as a boiler and storage cellar; the rest is a dry crawl space. The skeleton is the frame for the outer and inner walls. The columns and beams are partly hidden in the outer and inner walls, and partly free standing, covered with opaque glass. The steel skeleton is filled with masonry. The façades are composed of an outband brick wall finished with sand cement plaster that has been painted on the outside and treated on the inside with asphalt to keep out the damp. An unventilated 8 cm air cavity accommodates the stabilisers of the steel construction. The inside of the wall consists of light concrete or sometimes brick masonry. The masonry is underpinned by steel beams that are hung in the main supporting structure. The structural details show that everything has been done to prevent damp from penetrating the

cavity wall, and to protect the steel sections of the supporting structure and the joints of steel frames and window-sills against moisture. The way the awnings were built into the cavity of the steel sections is a detail that has been cleverly integrated in a technical and aesthetic way. The steel sections are protected at the top from the influence of weather by a steel plate and asphalt paper. These details reveal the combination of knowledge about how traditional and new building materials behave. It is also noteworthy how much attention and consideration must have been paid to the building physics of the constructions by Brinkman and Van der Vlugt. The choices they made at the time, however, are based on completely different energetic demands and performances from those that apply nowadays. Nevertheless, an explicit decision was made during the restoration to respect the technical physical organisation of 1933 as the basis because otherwise the well-conceived balance in the technical physical details of the time would be disrupted in an uncontrollable way. It is impossible to make this technically complex house satisfy present-day criteria consistently without doing fatal violence to the architecture.

A light concrete stone, and sometimes brick, has been used for the interior walls. Double walls have been used in places where sound had to be kept out, and noise insulation has been put in the floors. The indoor frames are made of steel and the plasterwork runs right up to the edge without any trimming.

A lot of attention has been paid to the installation and operation of the technical devices: the central heating, the sanitary fittings with their hot and cold

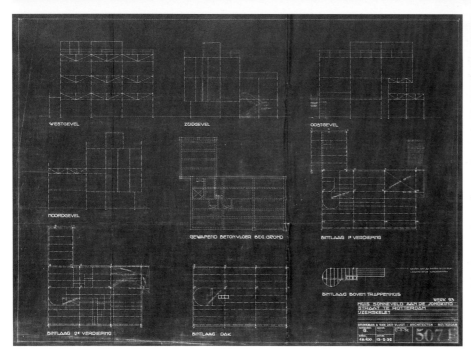

Blueprint of contract drawing
Brinkman and Van der Vlugt,
steel framed construction

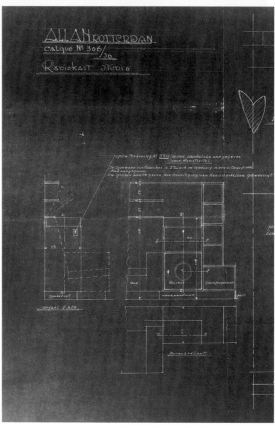

Blueprint of working drawing by
the Allan company for the radio unit
in the studio

water supply and plumbing, the electrical installation and lighting, the low-voltage apparatus with bells and light codes for the personnel, internal and external telephones, adjustable sound equipment with radio and gramophone in each room, two goods lifts and two garbage chutes for vertical transport. All these facilities have been fitted consistently into ducts and shafts throughout the house so that they can be accessed for maintenance. Switches and stopcocks have been fitted to the piping so that work can be done to the installation without having to switch it off in the whole house. This technically thought out and complete design of the house reveals the knowledge and experience that Brinkman and Van der Vlugt had acquired in industrial constructions, particularly for Van Nelle.

Research in the house

The observations carried out during the inventory stage were not enough to be able to determine the technical state of the house. Inspections by the restoration contractor, the structural designer and specialised companies were carried out soon after the start of the restoration activities to gain a good impression of the condition of the constructions and installations. This was of great importance for the research, especially to gain insight into the condition of the steel constructions; to find out the causes of visible defects,

to be able to detect any invisible defects, and to develop methods of restoration. A difficult dilemma emerged during this stage of the research. The walls were originally built from the outside to the inside, the exact opposite to the traditional construction of a cavity wall. This was done to be able to apply the layer of asphalt to the outside wall from inside to ensure that it was perfectly watertight before the inner cavity plate was blocked up. This procedure cannot be followed during the restoration because the finishing on the inside is already in place. However, it is impossible from the outside to ensure that the anti-damp layer is completely watertight in the original way. It was therefore decided to save the anti-damp layer if at all possible. It has only been broken where this was absolutely necessary. This called for a lot of problem-solving and inventiveness on the part of the parties involved, but it was necessary to prevent damage from damp in the future as a result of the restoration activities. The selection of the method to be used was decided on in each case by the creativity of the smith and the contractor in consultation with the structural designer and the architect. Whether the anti-damp layer could be saved or not depended on the depth to which the steel had been affected. Since the steel construction is riveted together and the stability of the house depends on steel girders contained in the façade, the steel components could not be dismantled. The damaged parts of the steel sections were removed and replaced by new welded sections. The general impression was that the extremely novel structural details of the time have stood up to the test of almost seventy years surprisingly well. 'The architects Brinkman and Van der Vlugt have ... proved that they are fully aware of their responsibility, and the way in which they apply new materials has a precision which compels the admiration of all', was the correct assessment of Ben Merkelbach in 1934![7]

The interior has also been subjected to the same cautious principle of restoration. The walls and ceilings were originally covered with prepared linen and emulsion paint. Every effort has therefore been made not to have to break this open, and the repair or replacement of installations has been carried out via the original, almost entirely intact ducts and system of shafts. A separate problem was raised by the restoration and reconstruction of the sanitary rooms with fittings that matched as much as possible. The de luxe foreign sanitary fittings that were originally applied in the house no longer exist and have not been found on the second-hand market. The tiles also have a different glaze and format to what is manufactured nowadays, and therefore had to be specially made. To replace missing sanitary fittings, the aim was to find models that were as close as possible to the originals and to install them in a way that closely followed the original method of installation. The reconstruction of the double sink in the kitchen, which was only taken out a few years ago, proved to be an extremely difficult task. There was nothing on the market that resembled the original of the wide glazed fireclay double sink brackets.

The electrical installation had been preserved in the house except for all the high-voltage switches. They were therefore specially made, as well as the various light fittings, for which it was easy to approximate the authentic form. The incorporation of the new security system was a difficult task. The new function of the premises as a monument that is open to the general public necessitates a number of present-day facilities. The members of the public are given the opportunity to walk freely around the house. This calls for an effective form of supervision that cannot be guaranteed by an attendant walking round. Closed circuit tv monitoring has therefore been adopted. It was also necessary to install modern equipment for burglary and fire prevention. These installations could all be incorporated without any disruptive interventions by making use of the original network of shafts, ducts and lowered ceilings.

A sense of authenticity

It is necessary to reconstruct the original state perfectly if the atmosphere, hygiene and comfort of this house are to be conveyed as clearly as possible. This model interior is still so close to what is regarded as a modern interior nowadays, as can be seen from the trade in remakes of Gispen furniture and classic sanitary fittings during the last few years, that the exclusive quality and characteristic mood of the house only come across if it is reconstructed in as pure a form as possible. The quality and luxury of the sanitary fittings, tiling, chrome and paintwork must be conveyed clearly. That is why the research paid special attention to the large amount of chrome metal and the many colours and textures that were applied in the interior. The colour research was carried out by the architectural office. For the chrome, advice was obtained from two metal restorers who drew up a plan of campaign to treat the chrome metal.[8]

The research investigated not only the exact specification of colour and material, but also the gloss and depth of the finish, the texture. The greatest care has been spent on maintaining original chrome layers, and much existing chrome has been cleaned, polished and conserved.

Preference was given to conservation because the damage and wear and tear of the chrome layer says something about the intensity of use, which in turn contributes to the sense of authenticity. That is why the door handles, for example, have been conserved as much as possible, even though the layer of chrome has worn thin.

Recording the knowledge and insights that have been acquired is an essential concluding stage of the restoration of this sculptural, architectural object with its remarkable personal and atmospheric interior. It throws new light on the architecture of Brinkman and Van der Vlugt and forms a source of inspiration for a reappraisal of the historiography of the architecture of the Modern Movement.

7   B. Merkelbach, 'Twee woonhuizen te Rotterdam van de arch. Brinkman en v.d. Vlugt', in: de 8 en Opbouw (12 mei 1934) 5, 77-81.
8   Jurjen Creman, furniture restorer, advised the Netherlands Architecture Institute to organise research on the composition and conservation of chrome and nickel on metal. This resulted in a report by Joostje van Bennekom and Susanne Meijer based on laboratory research conducted by the Netherlands Institute for Cultural Heritage in Amsterdam.

Colophon

This publication was made possible through the generous financial support of the **Stichting Volkskracht Historische Monumenten**.

Copy editing
Hermien Hamhuis
Barbera van Kooij
English translation
Peter Mason (essays)
Robyn de Jong-Dalziel
Image editing
Ingrid Oosterheerd
Lex Reitsma
Design
Lex Reitsma
Photography
Jannes Linders
    24, 64 top right, 74-108, 110-125, 127,
    128 bottom, 133, 135 left, 140-141, 145, 156,
    front cover
Other photographs
Fondation Le Corbusier, Paris
    51, 64 top middle
Gemeentearchief Rotterdam
    34, 36, 37 right, 38, 40
Historisch archief De Wed. Van Nelle N.V.,
Rotterdam
    46 top left, 63
Preservation of the Interior of
The Sonneveld House Foundation
    2, 6, 11-19, 32 bottom, 33, 42-44, 60 bottom,
    61, 62, 69-72, 109, 134, 135 right
© Jan Kamman / Netherlands Photo Archives
Rotterdam
    8-9, 28, 29, 66, 137, 148 bottom, 151 bottom
Netherlands Architecture Institute, Rotterdam
    22, 25, 30, 41, 46-50, 53, 56, 57, 60 top,
    64 bottom, 68, 128 top, 130-131, 136, 138,
    143, 148 top, 150 top, 151 top, 152, 153, 155,
    158, back cover
© Lucia Moholy-Nagy / Bauhaus Archiv, Berlin
    49 bottom left
© G. Rietveld / Stichting Beeldrecht, Amstelveen
    64 top left
SB4, Wageningen
    73
H. Voet Collection, Capelle a/d IJssel
    35 bottom middle
© Piet Zwart / Stichting Beeldrecht, Amstelveen
    10, 20-21, 23, 26, 27, 31, 32 top, 126, 132,
    149, 150 bottom
Drawings
Molenaar & Van Winden Architecten
Lithography and printing
Drukkerij Rosbeek, Nuth
Production
Barbera van Kooij
Publisher
Simon Franke

The Belgian consuls-general who lived in
The Sonneveld House

Frans Willems
1957-1964
Johan Naaykens
1964-1969
Lodewijk Vandenbrande
1969-1973
Alexander Van Mossevelde
1973-1977
Willem Verkammen
1977-1984
Andries Bouckaert
1984-1989
Karl Maenhout
1989-1992
Roger Martin
1992-1994
Hugo Fonder
1994-closure of the Consulate on
20 August 1996

The Sonneveld House was purchased for
the Belgian government by Mr Willems's
predecessor, Mr Grandy (who later became
permanent secretary at the Ministry of
Foreign Affairs).

Available in North, South and Central America
through D.A.P./Distributed Art Publishers Inc,
155 Sixth Avenue 2nd Floor, New York, NY
10013-1507, Tel. 212 6271999,
Fax 212 6279484.

Available in the United Kingdom and Ireland
through Art Data, 12 Bell Industrial Estate,
50 Cunnington Street, London W4 5HB,
Tel. 181 7471061, Fax 181 7422319.

Printed and bound in The Netherlands

ISBN 90-5662-197-1